The
Talk
in
Vandalia

JOSEPH P. LYFORD

1368

The Talk
in Vandalia

with photographs by the author

Harper Colophon Books
Harper & Row, Publishers
New York, Evanston, and London

This book was originally published by McNally and Loftin,
Publishers, Charlotte/Santa Barbara, in 1964,
and is here reprinted by arrangement.

First Harper Colophon edition published 1965 by
Harper & Row, Publishers, Incorporated,
New York, Evanston, and London

To
Philip Williams, Jr.
of Hinsdale, Illinois
1918-1942

Preface

Tragic events in our national life—the assassination of President Kennedy, the bombing of churches in Birmingham, the outbursts of hatred and violence in other cities—have caused many people to ask again what we Americans are and what we are becoming.

The development of the American character and the changing ways of Americans have fascinated observers and writers for centuries. We are indeed a peculiar people, engaged in an enormous experiment—an attempt to make democracy work on a continental scale, with a population composed of elements from all races and nations.

Four years ago the Fund for the Republic launched an investigation into the complexities of the American character. John Cogley, administrator of this project, organized a five-day meeting in Washington—a meeting that gave dozens of Americans of all varieties a chance to try out their ideas and argue with one another over what we were, what we were changing into, and where we were heading. Judges and doctors, theologians and psychiatrists, editors and publishers, sociologists and college students, government officials and historians, spoke freely and fully—often bogging down in difficulties, often contradicting one another.

Using some of the suggestions developed by that conference, Cogley asked a noted journalist—Donald McDonald—to conduct a series of long and searching interviews with knowledgeable persons active in many fields of American life—television, the press, the universities, science, stage and screen, opinion polls, the police, religious institutions, the law, architecture, and other areas of activity. These interviews, bearing critical comments by other intelligent and experienced people, were published as pamphlets and offered to the American public for a continuing course of self-examination.

Joseph P. Lyford, a Center staff member who had participated in the discussions of the American Character study, then came forward with an interesting proposal. He felt that the interviews had pretty well covered the views of "authorities" and "experts," but he wanted to find out what was going on in an American town. He sought an opportunity to talk with the "authentic, unknown citizens"—people who were not celebrities or major figures but were undergoing the stresses and strains of the 1960's in their own communities. The Center accepted his idea, and Cogley urged him to go ahead with it.

For his examination, Lyford picked a small middle western town. He chose a town in Illinois because he had grown up in that state and he felt he had some understanding of its people. He selected a community that was self-contained, not a suburb or a satellite of a large city.

He had four other factors in mind. He wanted to go into a town that was fairly even in its growth and fairly well-balanced in its industries, not dependent on defense spending or any single corporate business. He wanted a town with some historical atmosphere, some strong connection with the American past. He wanted a town in a transitional stage—not growing rapidly, and not steeply declining, but in a process of change. He sought a town that was changing but was not deeply involved in the racial crisis or any other overriding crisis which would distort or obscure its essential character.

So he settled upon Vandalia. He went to that small, solid community in Illinois with an open mind, a set of notebooks, and a tape recorder. He is a warm and friendly person, and the people of the town received him as an Illinois man who had returned to his home state for an inquiring visit.

The people talked, and he listened. In his report, entitled *The Talk in Vandalia,* he described what the town was like, what the people were concerned about, and what they had to say about themselves and their neighbors. He listened carefully, he thought about their problems and their opportunities, and he summed them up—clearly and frankly, without sentimentality and without malice.

When his report was issued as a part of the Center's study of the American Character, it stirred Vandalia and it stirred America. People all over the country recognized themselves in Lyford's pages.

The report dealt briskly and sharply with many of the problems of the town—but its special virtue was in its lively depiction of human beings. The businessmen, the farmers, the young teachers, the lawyers, the clergymen of various faiths, the students, the housewives, the doctors, spoke with the accents of reality about their daily struggle to do their duties, make a living, help their neighbors, and make sense out of the rush of events flooding over them. Lyford showed that the people of Vandalia did not fit into the Main Street folklore that had been built up around the rural towns of America.

"The talks in Vandalia do not support the American myth that a rural town today is a land-locked island inhabited by people who share an abiding complacency with each other," Lyford commented. "Vandalians today are in some ways in a better position to observe and to feel, sometimes most painfully, the consequences of a changing society than the suburbanite who lives in a bedroom town or the city dweller who hears about the world mainly from his newspaper and who enjoys the protective layers afforded him by his corporation, his union, and his various other institutional affiliations. There is also a special urgency in the air of Vandalia. A town on the edge of Chicago, Los Angeles, or New York City is forced to deal with the problems of sudden and uncontrolled growth, but Vandalia is beset by the much more desperate problem of how to hold on to what it has in order to survive."

The "special urgency" existing in the air of Vandalia evidently exists in other towns across America. Editors in Alabama, Arizona, Texas, Missouri, Michigan, California, Florida, New York, Rhode Island, and other states seized upon Lyford's report as a brilliant description of what was going on in *their* areas.

"The U. S. has many Vandalias," the *Arizona Daily Star* (Tucson, Arizona) said in a leading editorial. "As one reads Lyford's words, one realizes that there are many Vandalias—from Maine to California, and from the Canadian border to Florida." The Arizona paper urged its readers to purchase copies of the first edition of the book, made available to a limited number of readers by the Center.

Publisher's Auxiliary, a trade journal for newspaper publishers, declared: "It created more than discussion. . . . It created an uproar." The Chicago *Daily News* featured it on the front page, and the Houston *Post* ran nearly two full pages of excerpts from it. Describing it as "interesting, significant," the Dallas *News* said "it needs to be studied and matched by talk in Texas by citizens seeking honest, sound answers." The Montgomery, Alabama, *Advertiser* said "it is one of the few studies to plumb the real attitudes of farmers." It was reviewed and extensively discussed in the St. Louis *Post-Dispatch,* the Detroit *News,* the Providence *Journal,* the *New York Times,* the Miami *News, Newsweek,* and many other publications.

One of Lyford's statements in the book stimulated the Vandalians into action. He wrote: "It is strange to discover that an assembly of people who live together with a decency unheard of in a large city, and whose community efforts have been astonishingly successful, should at the same time lack the sort of serious communication with each other that would seem to be the basis of democratic life. The potential exists. Vandalia has an unusual assortment of sensitive and informed people. They have opinions, ideas, tempers. They would like to make their town better. But, given this, there is a reticence on important matters that is forbidding, and a lack of a forum—a New England-style town meeting, for instance—in which regular discussions could proceed."

The Vandalia newspaper and the Chamber of Commerce took up Lyford's challenge. A town meeting was held to argue about the points made by Lyford in his book. A thousand people turned up at the high school auditorium. Lyford spoke, and leading citizens replied to him. It was the largest meeting in the town's history.

Representatives of farm organizations, women's groups, lawyers, clergymen, teachers, and hundreds of other Vandalians and citizens of Fayette County hotly debated the town's future and the prospects for democracy in this revolutionary age. Cameramen for the National Broadcasting Company covered this debate, and correspondents for NBC News spent a week in the town, following up the repercussions. A special Chet Huntley Report, focusing on *The Talk in Vandalia* and the town meeting, was carried to millions of Americans over NBC stations in all parts of the country. The program set off another wave of discussion and argument in Vandalia and many other towns in the United States.

The hopes of Joseph Lyford and some leading Vandalians that this book would lead to the establishment of a permanent forum in Vandalia and other communities have not been fulfilled. The townspeople have not yet developed a series of ways to engage in serious communication about the deep problems that confront them.

But this book has affected, perhaps permanently, their accustomed patterns of thought and action. It is a book which deserves to be read and considered by all Americans who are concerned about what is happening to them and to their neighbors. It offers perceptive and vivid portraits of people who are worth knowing.

The life of an American town, caught in the torrents of a changing world, is presented here by a man who is an artist as well as a thoughtful, painstaking reporter.

FRANK K. KELLY
Vice President
Center for the Study of
Democratic Institutions

I

Judged by the map, the city of Vandalia (population 5,500) has a fine location. It lies across a junction of the Pennsylvania and the Illinois Central Railroads, appears to be the center of a criss-cross of highways, and is on the edge of the Kaskaskia River, which winds its way diagonally downstate to the Mississippi. But the map reader will be deceived. The Kaskaskia, swollen and icy in winter, subsides by summertime into a winding trail of mud and snags; the new superhighways—Routes 40 and 70—pass by to the north, and the only concession by the Pennsylvania's "Spirit of St. Louis" is a raucous bellow as it hurtles through a cut in the center of town an hour before noon. The Illinois Central is more considerate. Occasionally a freight engine shunts back and forth a few blocks outside of town to pick up some crates from one of the small factories along the tracks. "No trains stop here," the stationmaster says. The indifference of the railroads to Vandalia is paid back in full by the town's oldest practicing Democrat, eighty-eight-year-old Judge James G. Burnside. "We don't pay any attention to the railroads any more," he remarks. "They're just passing acquaintances."

A train traveler from the East can alight at Effingham, thirty miles away, trudge through the snow to the Greyhound Post House, and take the 1:30 p.m. bus, which is always overdue. The driver does not smile when along with a St. Louis ticket he gets a request for a stopover in Vandalia, which means that the express bus has to make a ten-minute detour off the main highway. Route 40 runs straight and flat as a tight ribbon through wide umber plains sheeted with winter rain, past farmhouses four or five to the mile. For a few hundred feet at a time the road will stagger and pitch slightly as the land wrinkles into prairie, creek, and brushwood; then it subsides again to a level as monotonous as the roar of the bus. The see-sawing pump of an occasional oil well is the only motion in the fields on a rainy day. There are a few crossroads villages, then the town of St. Elmo, and, finally, a few miles along Alternate Route 40, the city of Vandalia, once the western terminus of the Cumberland Road, capital of Illinois from 1819 to 1839, seat of Fayette County, and country of Abraham Lincoln of the House of Representatives of the State of Illinois.

The Evans is the taller, hotter, and more impressive of the town's two hotels. A fourth-story room offers a view of the magnificent old state house on the common, a tall-windowed white building, now a museum, where Stephen A. Douglas and Lincoln met with their fellow-legislators more than a century ago. The first-floor windows are not too far from the ground to have prevented a long-legged politician from swinging his leg over the sill when he wanted to make a quick exit. The town's second most noticeable monument is a huge, sand-colored statue of a pioneer woman who gazes down Gallatin Street's rows of two-story buildings, parking meters, vertical signs over a Rexall Drug Store and the Evans Hotel, past a pair of banks standing face to face at the main intersection, and, finally, across the tracks to the

Eakin Hotel, the County Courthouse on the hill, and one of Vandalia's many churches.[1]

Robert O. Hasler points out that the town has thirteen churches and ten lawyers. It is his business to know odd statistics because he is president of the Chamber of Commerce. He is handy to the main source of such information because his office is in the Town Hall just above the city clerk. Some time ago Hasler prepared a typewritten economic profile which begins, "Vandalia, centrally located in the heart of the Midwest, is seventy miles from St. Louis, ninety-five miles west of Terre Haute, 245 miles southwest of Chicago . . . total labor force of county 7,778, unemployed 276, self-employed 738, oil production 536. . . ." Under the heading of "Resources of Transportation" appears the information that on the Pennsylvania and IC railroads goods are "in transition" from Chicago, St. Louis, and Indianapolis—a politic way of saying that Vandalia is a way station. The figures on the sheets are from 1959, but Hasler says this is not a serious matter. "Things around here don't change very much from one year to another."

The township of Vandalia is grouped in three economic units. On its outer ring are the farms, the town's main support, ranging from sixty or eighty acres to several hundred, the average being somewhere in the middle. The chief crops are corn, soybeans, and livestock—mainly hogs and cattle. The land is worked with modern machinery by farmers who combine their own land with leased acreage—as much as they can get.

On the western edge of town are four factories, which employ altogether about 850 people. They are the Princess

---

[1] First Baptist, Second Baptist, First Methodist, Mother of Dolors (Catholic), Church of God, First Christian, Holy Cross Lutheran, St. James Lutheran, Assembly of God, Free Methodist, Pentecostal, First Presbyterian, Bethel Tabernacle.

Peggy dress factory; United Wood Heel, manufacturers of heels for women's shoes; the Johnson, Stephens and Shinkle shoe factory (the largest single employer with a work force of 475), and the Crane Packing Company, which turns out mechanical seals for automobiles, machines, appliances, etc.

At the core is the town itself—the stores, the banks, professional offices, churches, schools, filling stations, garages, plus the Elk, Mason, Moose, Odd-Fellow and Legion Halls, the Town Hall and County Courthouse, one movie theatre, restaurants, and nine of the only taverns in a county noted for its religion and its aridity. Vandalia's supermarkets are big and modern; its dry-goods stores range from the antique-looking Fidelity Clothiers to the Hub Department Store which has quality merchandise at New York prices. Only one commercial establishment—Radliff's Pool Parlor —remains open for business seven days a week. The local newspaper plant is built of yellow brick and houses the editorial staff of two weekly papers, the *Union* and the *Leader*. Most of the business district lies south of the Pennsylvania tracks except some hardware and feed stores, the Farm Bureau offices, and a cleaning establishment. On the north side of town the streets are lined with small frame houses, and a few large and attractive Victorian homes. Some blocks further out are the new County Hospital, the million-dollar Vandalia High School which is the community's pride, and a new development of luxurious, ranch-type homes. Beyond the high school is the intersection of Route 51 out of town and Route 40, which has given rise to a cluster of motels, restaurants, and filling stations. To the west lie the factories and on the far side of Shoe Factory Hill, along the Pennsylvania Railroad, are patches of dilapidated wooden dwellings which make up the hopeless part of town. To the east is the Kaskaskia River. The southern part of town peters out rather quickly a few blocks below the Post Office and the white frame house which is the home of Charlie Evans.

When he is not in the front parlor of his home, which he uses as his office, Mr. Evans is in the lobby of the Evans Hotel. He built the hotel in 1924 and, along with a hardware business and various real estate dealings, it made him probably the richest man in Vandalia. Last year, his eighty-first, the $106,000 library he gave to the town opened its doors. "We were a money-saving family, all of us," he says. "We're Welsh by descent. I was never a man to sell, I always bought and added to it. When I sold the hotel I'd been saving all the time. I guess I'd saved too much. I didn't have any use for the money, so I built the library. When I built it, I didn't try to cut corners. I didn't try to save as if I was building for myself."

Mr. Evans leans back, and crosses his arms when he talks about his town. "This is a historic city. When they moved the capital from here to Springfield in 1839, our population was only 400. We've gained a little bit all the time. Population-wise we've never had a setback. We've never had a boom. We held our ground. A big percentage of people own their own homes, including a lot who work at the factory. This makes us a good town for a factory. The companies know our workers are not fly-by-nighters. Their employees are here to stay. They have money invested in our town. Homes today build from $12,000 to $18,000, and we have a good building and loan program. Banks will lend money to anybody here who wants to build a building. We have good, sound, sincere bankers. Back in the late 20's, when people were trying to buy more and more land for their farms, the bankers warned them against it. When the crash came, we weren't so badly off as some. We had hard times in 1932, oh mercy.

"I think the town is going to develop pretty well. Rental

housing is pretty scarce. The homes here are good ones, and people have made substantial payments on them. I don't know what we're going to have to do to keep our young people here, though. When they go to the city, they don't come back. They want new people to get acquainted with. Industry might be the answer. We should have more opportunities for skilled workers. The Crane Packing Company has been very good. They have a training program for employees and they are expanding. The shoe factory is a shoe factory. Their idea is how much work you can get out of your help. It's as good a shoe factory as there is. It's a good town, but we have one bad problem. It's the farmers. The farmers are in trouble."

EVANS is not the only person who worries about the Fayette County farmers. The townspeople think and talk a great deal about them these days. They have always depended on them in the past, and they are no longer sure of them. The uncertainty may explain why the business of farming, traditionally honored in the State of Illinois as an independent way of life, is undergoing rapid sanctification. Probably more speeches are delivered at Kiwanis and Rotary clubs on the virtues and contributions of the tillers of the soil than on any other single subject; it is also the favorite topic of the county's political circuit-riders during campaign season. The community's businessmen prepare banquets in honor of local agriculture; the Junior Chamber of Commerce's first big dinner of 1962 was held to proclaim Siebert Hoover the "Outstanding Young Farmer of the Year" and present him with tickets to a Miami or New York vacation.[2] Agricultural experts from the University of Illinois and the Department of Agriculture, armed with pamphlets on fowl

_____

[2] Mrs. Hoover said she'd rather have a new refrigerator.

disease and hog pest, criss-cross the territory with advice on all phases of scientific farming. Secretary of Agriculture Freeman's emissaries from Washington are available to discuss the farm program at the smallest gatherings. The Farm Bureau offices have special classrooms where experts lecture local farmers and their wives on the economics of farm management. And, in contrast to the days of the Great Depression in other parts of the nation, the banker and the farmer maintain friendly, interdependent relations throughout Southern Illinois. The two bank presidents in Vandalia talk about farmers as if they were business partners and mutual allies under attack by the rest of the nation's economic interests.

The popularity of the farmer in the abstract has not always thawed out farmers in particular, some of whom still harbor ancient resentments against the town. (One farmer says he wants his children to stay in the rural schools because Vandalians think that "farm kids still piss on stumps and never heard of inside plumbing.") But many of the farmers seem to feel closer to the town than before the war, partly because of the knowledge that a lot of other people besides farmers are involved in their economic troubles, and partly because the farmers' own social life has become more and more interlaced with the life of the town. As the one-room rural schoolhouses have dwindled, over the farmers' opposition, from three dozen in the school district to a half dozen, farm mothers have become members of the PTA's of the Washington, Lincoln, and Central elementary schools. There is more talk in the homes of educational problems jointly shared with the townspeople.

Those farmers who work in the factories—"Saturday farmers," J. B. Turner, the county farm agent, calls them— have a growing association with non-farmers, and some even join labor union locals in the shoe and heel factories. Also,

the growing cost of running a farm because of the new machinery required and the rising prices of land have in-
creased the extent of the farmer's dependence on local
financial institutions. The farmers buy more and more of
their food locally—most of them have disposed of their dairy
cows and buy their milk at the Tri-City Supermarket and
the A&P. The farmer's machinery is repaired by local me-
chanics. Feed-dealer Norman Michel, who has carried a
few thousand people on his credit rolls, is a farmer's banker in his own way. Vandalia shapes its commercial activities
to suit the farmers' tastes, and the farmer, his wife and children, and his trucks are a regular part of the scenery on
Gallatin Street. This is not to say that the town has been
taken over by the farmers: in one sense it is the farmers who
have changed their habits and tastes—even in dress—to fit
the town.

The farmer has responded in other ways to the town. He
participates more in local events. He comes more to the
city's churches. One outstanding farmer is chairman of the
school district's Board of Education. Many of the more
prosperous farm families contribute their women's time to
fund drives. The high school's football and basketball
teams are getting a little more help from the farm youngsters who used to shy away from extra-curricular activities
after the last school bell. One still hears complaints from
the townspeople that the farmer is hard to reach, but he
is less and less remote.

Partly as a result of his accumulating difficulties, the political attitudes of the farmer seem to have become less distinct from those of his fellow-citizens in town. If anything,
his views on such matters as health insurance, social security, the United Nations, even labor unions, have often become more tentative than those of some of his city brethren.
The realization that government may be the only power

capable of restraining the technological and political forces gnawing at his economic position has affected the farmer's outlook considerably, and more than he will admit.

In matters of local politics, the farmer rarely finds himself at odds with the town, probably because politics in Vandalia is not a serious matter. The last great political controversy in the memory of the dean of Vandalia's lawyers, ninety-year-old Will Welker, was over temperance. Only on the school issue, not one that divides on party lines, does the farmer sometimes dig in his heels and refuse to budge. His stubborn desire to hold on to the one-room country schools defeated two attempts to float bond issues for elementary school construction in Vandalia. Even in this case, he was finally won over to support of the bond-issue program once he had the assurance that the rural schools would be allowed to continue. On those rare instances when a farmer talks world politics, his views are unexceptionably moderate on one side or other of the center: the voice of the John Birch Society is hardly audible in Southern Illinois.[3] President Kennedy, feared by many tight-jawed Lutherans and Baptists during the campaign as a possible threat to ancient Protestant values, is now spoken of mildly enough, and more often with praise than not.

The growth of the farmer's ties to his community, and the pleasant folklore of which he is the center, are not especially helpful to him in his present extremities, and this is true of farmers all over Southern Illinois. Businessmen's eulogies of the farmer's "way of life" seem to have become louder and more frequent in direct proportion to the approach of his economic doom. No amount of talk about how the farmer is the backbone of the nation alters the fact, as

---

[3] A chapter of Minutemen Guerrillas, organized in neighboring Collinsville, is regarded as a regional joke.

farmer Phil Gehle points out, that a tractor that cost him $1,600 in 1946 has a price tag now of $2,400, and that a bushel of corn in 1946 brought $2.25 as compared to $1.00 or less in 1962. The praise that rings in the farmer's ears has a little too much nostalgia in it to be entirely reassuring. It is almost as if he were hearing distant relatives discussing his virtues while he was being lowered into his grave. The farmers, least of all, have any illusion about the future. Those who remain on the soil around Vandalia live among ruins of abandoned farmhouses which are visible in almost any direction. The sturdy, independent way of life that makes Senator Dirksen's heart beat faster is rapidly becoming an anachronism in Fayette County.

The farmer's decline casts a cold shadow. Vandalia would suffer without its factories—their loss would be a fearful blow to the town's hopes for the future—but it could not survive without its farmers. As Dr. Josh Weiner puts it, "the job of people in town is to supply the farmer all the services he needs." Even the factories, with the possible exception of the Crane Company, depend heavily on the farmers and their families for their labor supply. Saddled with a heavy investment in farm machinery, the farmer must cultivate at least 250 acres or seek extra employment. Any less will usually not be enough to bring him the income he must have to pay his debts, maintain a household, and handle his interest payments to the farm-equipment dealer or the bank. So the small farmer turns to the heel and shoe factories for additional income, and often his wife and daughter work in the shoe factory or the dress factory. Without the "Saturday farmers" and their families, it is doubtful whether the plants could get their employees from any other large source at the $1.15 per hour that is the starting pay at all but Crane.

J. B. Turner, the county farm agent, a heavy man in his

sixties who looks like an unfrocked Southern Senator,[4] says that while Fayette County has 1,467 commercial farms, averaging 231 acres and bringing in a total income of over $13,000,000, nearly 500 people who live on these farms have other jobs as well. Almost half of them work 100 days or more a year in the factories, in the oil fields as servicing and maintenance personnel, and at the Norge plant in Effingham and the Caterpillar Tractor Company in Decatur, thirty miles away. The farmer is able to handle both a farm and a job because he is mechanized. Most of the farms have electrical equipment and modern conveniences; out of 2,100 county farmers who answered a poll by the University of Illinois, 1,400 had telephones and a slightly smaller number had freezers or refrigerators. Farmers own an average of two tractors apiece.

With all this capital equipment, the farmers are not getting any richer. It is estimated that the average net income of a Fayette County farmer is somewhere around $3,400 as compared to a state average of $4,500. But the fact that he has had to become more and more of a capitalist has certainly made his life more complicated. To stay afloat, he has to become a mechanic, an expert on governmental policies, a soil scientist, and a bookkeeper. For some, the economics and the competition have been too much. For others, farming has become distasteful because it has turned in a very few years into a totally different way of life.

In this new era a Vandalian who has become more and more important to the farmers is Harry Rogier, president of the First National Bank. His institution, and its competitor across the street, the Farmers and Merchants Bank, have never inherited the traditional rural dislike of the

---

[4] A misleading impression. Turner is a Republican with a tough carapace that enables him to hold his post even under a Democratic national administration.

money-lender. This is partly because there happen to be
some farmers in Rogier's own family tree—Rogier himself
grew up on a farm and still puts in many hours a week of
hard physical labor on his acreage before and after banking hours—and also because the financial decisions of his
bank have provided the underpinnings of a great many of
the surrounding farms. Rogier's bank, which has a "friend-
ship room" in the basement, complete with piano, for community use, is not cast in the cold, impersonal mold of
lending institutions which earned so much bitterness in
other parts of the country during the depression. The same
applies to the bank's officers. One vice-president, Dale Tedrick, is a leading county Democrat. He says that President
Kennedy's feed-grain bill is "the best thing that ever happened to the American farmer," and he often wears a
Franklin D. Roosevelt campaign button to banking con-
ventions.

As a matter of fact, most of Vandalia's bankers and those
in other rural Southern Illinois communities speak about
the economic policies of both Republican and Democratic
administrations in the past fifteen years with an impartial
bitterness and vehemence that has much of the flavor of
the old Populists. The recognized spokesman for bankers
like Rogier is the *Independent Banker,* which holds that
the farmer has been the victim of a conspiracy by every
organized economic pressure group in the society, and that
the farmer has "suffered the worst economic depression in
the history of the United States since the turn of the century."[5] The alliance of rural banks like Rogier's with the
farmers, who in Fayette County are largely a debtor class,
gives them a character quite unlike most banking enter-
prises in the East.

---

[5] "The 'Deliberate Debauchery' of Agriculture," by V. E. Rossiter, Sr. *Independent Banker,* February 1962.

"If we have a bad year, the bank will carry us along for a while until we have a chance to get back on our feet," says Fred Mattes, one of the community's most Republican— and most solvent—farmers. During the disastrous burn-out of 1954 the local banks outdid the FHA in its efforts to relieve the farmers' distress when their crops were pretty well ruined by a combination of scorching heat and a tornado that cut corn production to twelve bushels an acre. "There was a meeting of farmers in Greenville to talk the thing over. The bankers came and said that they would wait until next year for their loan payments if the farmers would just pay their interest charges." The "moratorium" was successful, and in a year transactions between banker and farmer were nearly back to normal.

THE First National Bank has a distinctly civic flavor. On Valentine's Day, for instance, coffee is served to the public, and the children of depositors are exposed to specially prepared incitements to thrift. A small table in the lobby is covered with small clay cat-and-dog coin banks. In another corner of the room is a collection of aluminum giftware, rewards for special savings programs. Bank executives walk about with red paper hearts pinned over their regular ones. In keeping with a hopeful view of the business cycle, the bank provides a Burroughs adding machine for the customers. High on the back walls of the lobby are mounted giant photographs of the Treasury Building, the National Capitol, and the Federal Reserve Building in Washington. Superimposed on the pictures are statements revealing numerous instances of government intervention in the bank business. "This bank is supervised by the U.S. government," is one proclamation; another, appearing on the picture of the Treasury Building, declares, "Headquarters, National Banking Department,

Our Supervisory Agency." A third announcement reads, "We are members of the Federal Reserve System."

Rogier is a chunky man with a face reminiscent of a small boulder. He makes it clear to visitors from the outside that he wants no part of anything that will hurt Vandalia, and he welcomes nobody who is bent on being a detractor. Once at ease, however, Rogier's conversation is candid and direct.

"We have had a revolution in this county, a revolution in agriculture. It has brought about a population loss. Vandalia has gained a bit, but the towns around have lost considerably. Maybe this is a sign we haven't done so badly. But nobody can tell. In the late 30's and early 40's we had an oil boom in the surrounding area, and it brought in a lot of people from Texas and Oklahoma. The wells made some local people rich. Rents went up. There was a great deal of business activity. But many of the people who came with the boom gradually left. We've been fortunate in getting some factories which have helped keep our population up, and this makes us a bit unusual among country communities around here. The level of our bank deposits is somewhat higher than in other towns, and we did benefit from taxes the county received from the oil companies. But in the next twenty years there will be a decline in income from this source and we have to think about something to take its place."

Like many others, Rogier is concerned about the decline in the farm population. "So many of the young people go away to live in Decatur, St. Louis, Springfield, and Chicago, and when we lose a farm family the banks and the retail stores lose a whole family of customers. We've had to make a great many concessions to develop new employment opportunities. When the word got out that the United Wood Heel was coming to Vandalia, there were

600 applications for less than 150 jobs. It meant that more and more farmers were beginning to look around. It isn't surprising. It's gotten harder and harder for them to rent land, not just around Vandalia, but all over the state. This means that when a farmer has two or three boys, there isn't any chance for all of them to remain on the farm. The father can't subdivide because the smaller the farm gets the more uneconomical it is. So one boy may take the farm, and the others move away. This farm situation is a problem for our high school, too. The boys who cannot go on to college have to go somewhere from school, and the old roads to jobs are closed, so it means a new type of training for them. I think our schools ought to give more and more vocational training. We ought to make a survey of the industrial possibilities in this area and figure out some way of planning a training program for them in the schools.

"If the farmer is having rough going it isn't because he can't get credit," Rogier adds. "Most of the farmers are tied to the banks, while others get their money from the Farm Home Administration at a slightly lower rate of interest. A large part of our money is invested in loans to the farmers, usually for operating expenses. There is also a production credit association, a cooperative that gets money from the government and then lends it to the farmers. The government has been able to help the farmers in many ways. But there is the old trouble with federal agencies. They begin as a temporary means of dealing with an emergency, but the emergency never ends. The bureaucrats never give up."

The almost automatic dig at the federal government that one hears from many farmers and businessmen like Rogier seems to have little relation to their economic behavior. The farmer who speaks sourly, if without any real passion, about "government hand-outs" is almost invariably willing to go along with the soil bank and feed-grain programs and to avail himself of the technical and advisory services of the Department of Agriculture and the University of Illinois's extension program.

Rogier explains the seeming contradiction between the farmers' verbal and actual responses to federal assistance by saying that "farmers are opportunists like everyone else. When someone wants to give us something, we take it. Most of the farmers use the Agricultural Stabilization Conservation Program, which helps provide limestone and phosphate to improve the soil. Of course some farmers won't take it; they don't believe it's right to take things from the government. But other farmers have weakened gradually and now they go along. Their attitude is that we're helping to pay for these programs, so why not get some of the benefits?"

Rogier acknowledges that there are situations in which the government is needed, and that there is disagreement among the farm organizations on what attitude to take toward the federal programs. One program, for example, that Rogier feels is necessary is a freeze of the dairy farmers' milk prices at last year's level so that they can "achieve a little stability." Many of them are going out of business, and this might give them some sort of production control. Rogier also advances the view that, in Illinois at least, "the conservative and wealthy farmers who oppose government help to the farmer are the ones who are really on the side of revolution." The economic and technological factors that have revolutionized farming in the area are working for the bigger and richer farmers by driving the small operators out of business; any government action that tends to slow this consolidation arouses their opposition.

In his office, confronted with the problem of protecting the economic stability of his customers, Rogier wastes little time on McKinleyisms. To some extent he seems to share the farmers' subconscious change in attitude towards the role government may have to play not just with relation to the farmers' own immediate price problems, but in the nation's economy as a whole. Like the farmer, he recognizes that the farmers' costs are directly related to the great union-management negotiations in steel and autos, and that these power groups are able to make mutually satisfactory agreements that can wipe out the profit margins of thousands of farmers. Rogier is not the only local businessman to admit that what some businessmen call "socialistic" activities of government may help preserve some semblance of competition among conflicting economic interests. In most discussions of price and wage controls with Vandalians like Rogier or Phil Gehle, a farmer who is just as conservative as Rogier, there is an initial resistance to any such idea, but if the question is asked, "Should wages in the steel industry be controlled?" or "Should corporations be subject to some sort of check in their pricing policies?" the reactions become varied and contradictory.[6]

While not necessarily typical, Rogier's attitude is instructive. "Other groups, unions and management, can set their prices and operate under some reasonable assumptions. And when they set their prices, they don't have to worry about how it affects anybody but themselves. But some farmers can't ever know their prices in advance— sometimes it takes a dairy farmer forty-five days after delivering his milk to find out what price he got. He can't

---

6 In speaking about the steel industry, Rogier will usually concentrate his fire on the unions, but he acknowledges that "maybe the steel companies should be blamed" for their April 1962 attempt to raise steel prices $6 per ton. "It's hard to understand how the companies, with all their high-paid public relations men, could make such a mistake." Rogier is also split in his instincts about President Kennedy's intervention against the price rise. "I deplore what he did, but, then again, maybe we need legitimate pressures on both unions and management to control inflation."

wait to see what the price is, and even if he could, he wouldn't be able to hold off if he didn't like it. So there he is, a seller in a buyer's market, and a buyer in a seller's market when it comes to farm implements.

"I'll certainly admit that if it hadn't been for government controls on milk prices there would have been a disaster in our agriculture. Now the farmer who doesn't want to sell at current prices can get a loan from the government to operate his farm while he stores his grain for a better market. We certainly don't want to go back to the old days of the depression. Plenty of farmers still say it's immoral to take any help. But if you talk to an ordinary dirt farmer he'll tell you that if it hadn't been for the government he would have been ruined long ago."

IVAN SNYDER, a general farmer in Shafter Township, is one of those who live perpetually on the margin of extinction. He drops down off a mud-spattered tractor which he has been driving with his two boys. He is a dark-haired 200-pounder, about forty years old, dressed in blue coveralls and the ubiquitous visored cap. He has a quick but nervous smile. Snyder farms a total of 215 acres, some of which he owns and some of which he leases under an arrangement, like that of other farmers, whereby he pays the landlord 40 per cent of the income from the leased property and shares the cost of seed and fertilizer. He does not have to grope for words to express his situation.

"I don't know whether to buy more land or not. I've got to have it to stay in business, but I can't afford the price. It's gone from $50 to $300 an acre, and even then you can't find land to buy. The doctors and lawyers are buying it up and renting it out. I've been in debt clear up to my ears. The interest on my loans is eating me up and if I don't expand my acreage I'm licked. The cost of carrying a tractor and corn picker and sheller and a truck is just the same, whether I'm farming 200 acres or 600. I've been in debt every year since 1956. My land isn't enough to support my family. I've got four more besides those fellows [pointing to his sons]. The boys want to be farmers and I've tried to talk them out of it. This is a hard thing for me to do, to tell my oldest son he can't do the thing I wanted to do when I was his age, especially when he has the making of a good farmer—they gave him an aptitude test at the high school and found out he was best at mechanical things and ought to farm. What should I do—tell him to look for another kind of job he can't do as well, a job that doesn't even exist? It takes as much money to start a farm now, with all the equipment we have to have and the prices of feed and fertilizer, as it does to start a good business—$15,000 to $20,000. Where can they get that kind of money? A kid can't start farming these days the way he used to. The only way he can make it is to have his old man turn over everything he has to him free and clear. I'm pinned down. It's been real bad this year, the worst I've ever seen."

Snyder is one of the many farmers who didn't get all of his crops out of the fields before the winter rains that flooded the frozen ground.

"Farming is nothing but a big business now. My dad worked only eighty acres and he did pretty well. All he needed was some horses and his sons to help with the work. He didn't owe any money. It was a good and decent life for a man who wanted to be his own boss. Now you starve to death on eighty acres—even on twice that much. People who live a thousand miles away talk about how the government is propping us up. What can the government do for me? I get 89 cents a bushel for corn, which is about half of what it used to be.

"We've tried every way to beat this thing. I've bought

some livestock, thinking maybe if I could get a spread of animals I could get along with a little less land and equipment. My wife went to work in the shoe factory for a while and it damn near drove us both crazy. I was making the kids' lunches and getting them off to school in the morning, and when she came home she was dead tired. If I could keep my boys with me, we could work the fields and plow and plant at the same time. Maybe I could have gotten my corn out in time if I'd had them both. But how can I ask my boys to work for me when they're out of school no matter how much I need them, the way things are?

"You remember the depression? I remember it, even though I was only a kid. Was it any worse than it is today? What's the difference? The only difference is that today you can borrow money and go into debt a little deeper. People talk about the farmer being independent, how he doesn't work for anybody but himself. There's nothing independent about me. The farmer works for the grain dealer and the fertilizer dealer and the fuel dealer and the banks. They've got it all.

"Yes, I've thought of giving up. But how does a farmer give up? Where does he go? They don't want a man my age, who doesn't know anything else. Do I just walk into that house and tell my wife I'm quitting tomorrow? I had a friend who sold out and bought a house in town. He thought he could get a job. He had six children. That means he had to have at least $85 a week to live. He looked all over town for some kind of job. They wouldn't even talk to him. Finally he bought a filling station. What a hell of a way that is for a man to die.

"Quit?" Snyder shrugged. "I can't quit until they make me."

There are as many kinds of farmers as there are farmers. Not all of them are in Snyder's predicament. Some began with an inherited farm, with good land, buildings, electricity, and plumbing. Others have had another sort of luck, a piece of land over the oil that was discovered in the late 1930's. Some farmers were able to buy land before the war when it could be had for a fifth of its present price. Then there is the matter of a little specialized education. It has helped a man like Leo Murray, an Air Force pilot who can buy used machinery because he is a good mechanic and can do all of his own tinkering without fear of a breakdown during the harvest or plowing seasons.

Murray is a straight, slender man with a lean face, pale blue eyes, and a wide smile. If any farmer has visible means of sturdy support, he has. First, in his dark-haired wife who scrubs and polishes her house, and in six lively small children. Second, in a farm that looks as neat and efficient as a clock. Third, in his knowledge of how to coax and baby the machinery that is the tool of his survival.

Murray owns his equipment and land free and clear. He has thought, but "never seriously," about giving up on his 118-acre farm (which, with his leased acreage, totals a healthy 318 acres) on which he raises wheat, corn, beans, hay, and some livestock.[7]

"My big problem is finding land to rent. It's so scarce you almost have to buy these days, and this means $50,000 or $60,000 for a decent-sized farm. I've been lucky so far because my landlady is an elderly woman who seems to be satisfied with our arrangement. But I can look around at other farmers who don't know from one year to the next when their leased land will be sold out from under them to someone—very often someone who isn't a farmer. No matter, I'd rather take my chances than work in a factory. You can work there every day of your life and come up with

---

[7] Just recently Murray indicated he means to stay in business by borrowing money to buy another parcel of farmland.

nothing in the end. I'm not too proud to work for somebody else, but I figure I'm as smart as he is, so why shouldn't I work for myself?"

Murray looks straight at his wife when he talks. "I'm thinking there should be more stock raised in this country. This is more for grazing, different from up north where I came from, where the land is black. We've had to figure close on things because we started in this neighborhood from scratch. My brother has my dad's farm. A lot of the people here start with an advantage. They inherit a farm. I was just lucky that I knew a woman who would rent me land down here."

There is an air of hope in his house. Mrs. Murray likes it here. She thinks that it is fine for the children. One boy has some registered sheep, and he's doing well at Vandalia High School. His mother likes the rural school nearby better than the overcrowded elementary schools in town. Murray is head of the rural school's PTA. By dint of some high-pressure cake sales and other fund-raising devices the PTA bought the school a screen and a slide projector. The fathers made physical education equipment for the youngsters, such as a jumping pit and a chinning bar. The parents would like to do something about getting indoor toilets for the school. If Murray's children show an interest, the parents will try to send them to college, "if we can make it financially." The older boy likes farming. He has also thought about becoming a veterinarian, which would mean two things working for him on the farm, since there aren't many vets nearby. The Murrays have to call Nokomis, thirty miles away, when they need one. The other son has no intention of being a farmer. "He likes book work," says his father, pleased.

Occasional clouds pass over the Murrays' good humor; for instance, when they talk about how doctors and lawyers are getting control of more and more of the land. "They're the real capitalists in our part of the state," Murray remarks. "Just look around. Who drives the Cadillacs? It's the doctors." Mrs. Murray speaks up. Cadillacs *per se* aren't what bother her. "Someone in our family had the flu a few weeks ago. They charged her $17.50 a day for a bed in a four-bed ward in Taylorville. Farmers don't get higher prices, but hospitals and doctors are raising their prices every day. It costs $360 to have a baby in the Decatur hospital." Her husband says, unsmiling, that $360 is his net profit on 1,000 bushels of corn, the yield of more than ten acres. It also represented about five weeks' pay for Murray when he worked at the Crane Packing Plant during one of his "tight periods."

The anger passes because the Murray children have joined the conversation. One nice thing about being a farmer, it is suggested, is that he can always be around his wife and children. Murray laughs out loud, "Yes, they're on my back all the time." His German neighbors know Murray's mixture of stubbornness and humor. When he first settled here, he says, they would remark laconically, well, we had an Irishman here once, but he didn't stay long. Their new neighbor would answer, "There will be a lot of you folks gone before I leave." His prediction has already come true.

ONE of Murray's German neighbors is Anton Matzker. If there are seasons in a farmer's fortunes then Matzker is in his summer. There is a special kind of health to his farm. It has the feeling of a principality, off on a side road and past some hills. The land spreads far off on either side of the road to the farmstead, and in the distance are some palisades of trees. Even on a late winter afternoon the air seems to have a touch of warmth. The grey Matzker house, a clump of outbuildings, and tall trees are grouped in a pleasant island. The fields are the prosperous color of silver.

A hundred yards away, near one of his outbuildings, the farmer is working with some cattle. "I'm Matzker, or what's left of him," he says as he walks over through the mud. He looks across the fence without expression, a man in his fifties with an open face and grey eyes. Why have I come there? Is that your car in my driveway? Who has driven me to his farm? There are many more questions. Finally he gazes at the ground for twenty or thirty long seconds. Then he swings over the fence and walks toward my car: "I'll talk to you."

Matzker is a man who has won most of his struggles with the land and who has a farm now that is sound and secure and will produce what his family needs for the rest of his days. Matzker was born on this place, and his father before him. For nearly a hundred years it has been in the family. It was big when he inherited it and he has made it bigger. He has good strong buildings, some made with his father's hands, and he has made them stronger and added more buildings. The house has been refaced and the fences repaired.

Matzker owns 280 acres and he leases 200 more. He has three tractors, a pusher combine, some beef cattle, hogs, and a few chickens. He has some wasteland for pasture, and he grows hay for feed. His cattle go to market in the spring. The chief crops are corn and soy beans. Matzker has never signed up in the government's soil bank program, not because he has any great objection to the government's helping the farmers—"Washington has done some good things" —but because he thought last year he could make more money using all his corn acreage than by taking his allotment out of cultivation.

"Maybe I would have been better off if I had gone into the soil bank," Matzker laughs. "We had the wettest winter I can remember, and I didn't get all my corn out." But prospects aren't discouraging. Matzker has a son who is a Future Farmer of America. "There's his test patch out back there. We doctored it up with all kinds of fertilizer and the boy got a high check of 139 bushels per acre on the plot. He'll be pretty well set when he gets out of school, I guess, with a farm like this to take over." The tendencies of the other five Matzker children haven't been observed. Three are attending a two-room rural school in Vera.

Matzker is a rare farmer in this area. He can watch his neighbors disappear without having to wonder when his turn will come. He sweeps a finger in a slow full circle pointing into the distance and ticks off the names of farms, just out of eyesight, that have been abandoned. "Farming is a gamble, the sort of gamble you can't resign from until they've chased you out or you're worn out for keeps. There isn't anything in between winning out or losing everything."

But even Anton Matzker still has some battles left to fight. A year ago he spent two months in the hospital, and he hasn't yet regained his strength. Until his son is ready to help he will have to go on handling the farm alone, except in the rush times at plowing, planting, and harvesting. Then, despite his extra help, he will straddle a tractor twelve to fourteen hours a day, for a ninety- to hundred-hour week. Even in the summer of his fortunes, there is no time to rest.

If and when it comes, retirement is neither tranquil nor easy, even for a farmer who has won his battle, usually because he is so accustomed to work that he cannot force himself into inactivity. Clifford Hoffman is an example. He lives near the border of Vandalia and Shafter townships.

He is sixty-nine years old. Standing in an icy wind, near his garage, he says he has "retired." "I have just twelve acres of corn and some beans, and a little poultry and livestock. I don't do much. I have arthritis, for one thing." Hoffman's yield of corn last year was 110 bushels per acre. Although he and other farmers cut back their acreage and put it in the soil bank, he still had a bigger total yield of corn than in previous years because he "doctored" his cultivated land heavily with fertilizers. While Hoffman is pleased that he was able to raise his production, he obviously feels a bit uncomfortable about the soil bank. He thinks it probably isn't a very good idea for the government to be in the price-support business, but he admits that there isn't much agreement among farmers on this point. Hoffman is also impressed by what seems to him to be the government's illogical financial support of farmers who clear brush land for cultivation at the same time it is trying to withdraw land from corn and wheat production. In spite of all the government activity, he says, "the farmers as I knew them are disappearing. They're becoming tenants of doctors and lawyers and business people who are buying up the land around here. Farming is a job for a capitalist now, and, even then, you are lucky to get 2 or 3 per cent on your investment."

Hoffman turns his thoughts upon the past. He says that when he was a young man he made a very good living on his own 150-acre dairy farm. It was one of the best in the country. But one day he decided to become a country preacher. Why? "Because God called me." So he gave up a good part of his herd, and his wife and son ran the farm while he was visiting his rural Baptist congregations. He would leave on a Saturday afternoon for his ministry and not come back until Monday evening. He says that if there is a reward in heaven for anybody, it should be for the small family that took care of things while he was away. Sometimes his revival tours lasted for three weeks.

"I still get letters from people who were saved. It makes all the hard things that went before worthwhile. I was blessed with a family that gave me support when I was in need. The farmer today doesn't have his family by him so much any more," he says. He sees the wives driving down the Shafter Road at 6:30 in the morning on their way to work at the shoe factory. "In the old days the mother could be with her children, where she was most needed, and the father would always be nearby, even if he was out in the fields in the day."

When the roads, the weather, or his arthritis, or all of them together, are acting up, Hoffman can telephone his Baptist meeting—thirteen people in all—and they allow him to stay home. If his congregation can't make it, some- one calls him and lets him know. The rest of the time Hoffman works on his chicken house, feeds his livestock, and plows, plants, and picks his corn. Sometimes the man who began farming as a small boy behind a country plow visits the son who runs a good farm to the north with trac- tors, corn-pickers, trucks, and a combine—the same son who helped his father many years ago. And on these trips Hoff- man's wife, who still keeps house and tends the chickens, goes with him.

IN another part of the township, to the west of Vandalia, is John Daniels, a farmer with a business- man's way of doing things. He also takes a leading part in the affairs of his community. In his forties, blue-eyed, with a body as solid as one of his own tractors, Daniels is chair- man of the Vandalia Board of Education. Together with Vandalia's Vicki Nutter, who became Miss Illinois a few years ago, Daniels is one of the community's two national celebrities, having twice been national plowing champion. His attractive brunette wife, Christine, has also done her stint with the school system. During the war she engaged in a sort of simultaneous educational chess by teaching six grades at once in a rural schoolhouse.

If the strength of a farmer's optimism is directly related to the condition of his farm the fact that Daniels's farm of 555 acres is one of the most prosperous in the county undoubtedly explains why he is more hopeful about the future than many of his neighbors. He does not feel that the general farm is going to have to get bigger and bigger in order to survive, and he believes in the future of the small farm, which would specialize in certain types of livestock, thereby eliminating much of the expense of heavy mechanical equipment and freeing the farmer from a continual quest for added acreage.

In 1955 Daniels got what amounted to a surprise postgraduate course in agriculture when he traveled to Sweden to participate in the World Plowing championships (he was awarded eleventh place). "The farms were small, around sixty-five acres on the average, and the specialties were dairying, beef, pork, and chickens. The Swedish farmers didn't have the high prices we have, but this didn't explain the amazing success of these farms. Each farmer did one thing, scientifically and intensively. One small farm had 3,000 hogs, for example. The government has a program to do everything it can to encourage development of a sensible farm system, based on scientific techniques and business knowledge. There is very little export. Here, in Vandalia, too many farmers rely on crops, which is bad because land is getting so scarce. But the important difference in Sweden is that the government subsidizes farmers to produce more, not less. The farmers are producing more and more for their own countrymen, not less all the time.

Why can't we learn something from this? The hungry people aren't all concentrated in Europe or China. Hungry people are here, too, but we don't worry about them. We say surpluses are a problem. Why is that the problem? If everybody were fed, the surpluses would take care of themselves. I can't understand why we would rather take land out of cultivation and store grain than give it to people who need it." [8]

Daniels is a Democrat who feels that there has to be some control of farm production, but he is struck by the great confusion among farmers about the nature of frequently changing government programs. The Farm Bureau, the Farmers Union, and the Grange all disagree on the basic issues of farm policy, Daniels remarks. "How can you get anywhere when the three farm organizations can't get together, especially when the farmers, even if they did cooperate, would be a minority? The situation seems even more hopeless when you see what the labor unions are doing. The fact is that the farmer can't organize. If his cattle are ready, they have to be taken to the market and sold. That is true of hogs and corn, too, although corn can be stored if the farmer has the facilities. Holding on to hogs for a month after they are in prime condition fattens them and cuts their value. The farmer doesn't have the bargaining power of the steel company, which can stockpile steel, or the unions, which can strike. Except for grain, it is almost impossible for him to withhold his product."

Daniels tells about a farmer's cooperative that attempted to get all its members to withhold their hogs in order to keep the prices up. Members who tried to sell their hogs before the time set by the union were to be fined 10 per cent of their sale price by the union. In one such case a

---

[8] Daniels suggests that some of the government surplus be given to CROP, a private organization that distributes free food to needy families overseas.

man driving hogs into St. Louis was stopped by the co-op's inspectors, told not to sell. He said, "I have a $5,000 note here due tomorrow. If you'll lend me the $5,000 I'll take my hogs back home." They wouldn't lend him the $5,000, so the farmer had to sell his pigs.

Will the farmer ever get over his feeling of guilt about taking government help? "The farmer is going to have to answer this problem himself. The question is, what does he want to accomplish? The government can't do anything for the farmer unless the farmer himself has a plan and has a desire and the energy to go ahead." Daniels cites examples of how farmers have signed up to cooperate with the district soil conservation program. The Department of Agriculture people will help the farmer write out a farm plan, show him how to plow in strips, to control erosion by contour plowing. This is a free service, "but it is not a handout because the farmer must be willing to do the work and invest money." Daniels has done a great deal of strip and contour plowing. He has torn out his old fences and replaced them with permanent fences of multiflora rose bushes. Contour plowing prevents fertilizer as well as soil from washing down into the lower fields. "Some farmers have to get over the idea that gullying is the only problem. They have trouble dealing with problems that are not visible to the eye. A farmer will get upset about gullying, but he won't do much about the washing away of fertilizer because he doesn't see it."

There are many services available to the farmer through the soil and wild life conservation program, Daniels says. "If you have the initiative to plan and work out new things for the farm you can make out all right. Every farmer has a different feeling about his farm and what he's up to, what he ought to do." Instead of giving money to the farmer, Daniels feels the government can do best by giving knowledge and technical advice. He said it's a little bit like what our foreign aid program ought to be, that is, aid to under-developed countries.

"I think we've made a mistake in giving great amounts of money to these countries which are not really in a position to use it because of their relatively primitive level of organization. What we need are people who understand these countries, who understand the educational shortcomings of the people, their culture, their background, and their economy, and who can make sensible recommendations for technical assistance. This is helping them to help themselves."

"It's too bad farmers can't travel more," Daniels says. "Everything abroad seems to be the reverse of the way things are done in this country. It would shake us up a bit and give us a new way of looking at things."

Daniels feels that his community has turned its face away from world problems, and that Vandalia and other towns are hurt by this attitude. "A lot of people I talk to still don't think the United States could be bombed in a war." With such an attitude it is no wonder that there is complete apathy about civil defense. "There is a bit more realism in a town like Carbondale, where you have a college [Southern Illinois University]. People are exposed to the world there, in some degree. There is a group of very interesting teachers from abroad. I talked for a long time to a young Peruvian and a boy from Kenya, and it opened my eyes. The Kenya boy's tribe has only about one educated person in every 100,000, and the most important thing in the world to them is to get into a group where somebody can read to them. The whole tribe chipped in to send the teacher to the United States, and was able to raise just $400. Educated people are so scarce that there are just a few of them at the top. Educational facilities are so limited that by the third or fourth grade children are taking exams at regular periods which they have to pass if they are to go on. The exams continue right up through college. It's impossible for us to imagine the tremendous drive to get an education in a place like Kenya. What bothers me is that if so-called primitive nations in Africa understand that education is a life-and-death matter, why is it so hard for us to place a proper value on education in our country?"

Daniels has a whole forest of plowing trophies in his living room, but he seems proudest of his prizes for soil conservation, and an etching of a landscape in Uppsala, Sweden. In the distant background is the spire of the church where Dag Hammerskjold is buried.

EMIL MOSSER, the agricultural expert from the University of Illinois who conducts classes in farm management at the Farm Bureau offices, says that the farmers are about the only real entrepreneurs left in our society. Daniels, Phil Gehle, and Fred Mattes are the types he has in mind; men who plan, administer, keep accounts, study new production techniques, and run their businesses with their own money and credit. They are not a common breed in a nation where more and more men and women work at jobs with steady pay, shorter hours, pensions, medical benefits, and paid vacations. These are inducements the young man in a farm community finds it harder and harder to withstand, especially when measured against the doubtful pleasure of being one's own boss in a sinking economy.

Yet, despite the swallowing up of small farms, a good proportion of Vandalia's farmers act as if they can survive the revolution. Farmers of German ancestry are especially stubborn about holding on to their land, often selling it for less than market price to a relative so as to keep it in the family. The farmers treat their land not just as a business but as a family treasure which has been built up by many generations. Harry Rogier says that farmers rarely go into bankruptcy voluntarily, no matter how serious their situation.

Why the tenacity? The fact is that, unlike many of his fellow-Americans, the farmer likes the community in which he lives and he wants to stay there. He is not about to become one of the migrants to the city if he can help it. And just as often, he has a son who wants to stay and is learning more about agriculture by the time he is fifteen than his grandfather learned in a lifetime. The farmer values the sort of family organization that a farm life imposes, where the welfare of every member is of immediate concern to every other and affects the livelihood of all. "And where else can a kid grow up where he can have his own horse and cows and chickens and pigs, and get up early and go out on the tractor with his old man? Where he has a pond in his back-yard full of blue gill and catfish he can catch any time he wants to bait a hook?"

Another reason the farmer hangs on, Fred Mattes says, is because he's a conservative—"He's got to be: he has to figure close." He can't afford to switch around like a factory worker because he has everything tied up in his work. But he is also a gambler, who never can know the odds against him. "You decide how you're going to use your land, you put something in it, and then watch it grow," Phil Gehle says. "You watch and wait, and if you come out right, you've got something."

The very development of mechanization, which has been the destruction of many and the constant peril to those who remain, has also emancipated the farmer. It has made him the most efficient farmer in the world in terms of what he can get out of his land. It has given him time off for a good part of the year, leisure being something he never had twenty years ago. Ivan Snyder's father, who worked a farm of eighty acres, made it pay, but he had to do it with horse-drawn plows and live in a farmhouse with kerosene lamps, no plumbing, no telephone; he lived in isolation in winter and in the rainy spring months when he could not fight his way out along the muddy trails that were all he had for roads. Today the tractor, combine, truck, and corn picker have finally made it possible for a man to dominate his land and develop new types of activity. He is learning to use and take care of machinery because he has to, but it also gives more diversity to his life. Because of the changes in farm operation, the farmer can be more a part of his community, contributing to it and sharing some of the things it has to offer.

For the Vandalian farmers who remain on their land, the future, for a generation at least, does have some promise—more than it had for their grandfathers. It is ironic that so many should be losing out at the moment when a quiet revolution has put them in reach of a better life.

II

: It would be misleading to say that
Vandalia takes everything in its stride, because "stride"
implies a measured forward movement which has never
been a community characteristic. It is also inaccurate to
take the community's easygoing manner at face value. Its
calm demeanor is sometimes achieved at the cost of sup-
pressing grave internal discontents. Nevertheless, the atmosphere is rarely charged with the type of emotional
storms that test the tempers of New York or Chicago
suburbanites. The political fracases that periodically rock
a Westport, Connecticut, to its foundations, setting com-
muter against ancient inhabitant, are unknown. Public
controversies usually do not get past the stage of fairly low-
pressure arguments over personalities or such transient irri-
tations as disintegrating sidewalks and sheriffs. Candidates
do not run for municipal office, they file for it, on ballots
that do not mention party affiliations. The only lively competition recently was for the job of county sheriff, but the
plenitude of aspirants was attributed to a rise in the unem-
ployment rate, adding considerable glamour to the sheriff's

$5,000 yearly stipend.[1] The community blood pressure is unaffected by animosities between Republican and Democrat. County administrations alternate between the two with regularity, and the towns do not even have local political organizations.

The campaign for mayor is not usually one of Vandalia's most exciting events. Last year's canvass was enlivened somewhat when one candidate promised that, if elected, he would fire the police chief. The reformer was elected, but the police chief is still police chief, and there have been no outraged cries from the electorate about broken campaign promises. It is understood that it is pretty hard for a mayor of Vandalia to fire anybody. It is also generally known that Norman Michel didn't really have his heart set on being mayor, anyway. Although he refrains, out of civic pride, from saying so publicly, there is reason to believe that he considers the mayor's job a trivial and unremunerative demand on time that could have been better spent handling the complicated affairs of a successful feed and grain business. In return for enduring the burdens of the town's highest administrative office, Michel receives $1,200 yearly, considerably less than the earnings of each member of the two-man squad that issues from the Town Hall each day to empty nickels from the parking meters. The mayor's perquisites include neither a black limousine nor office space in the Town Hall.

A discussion with Michel in the back office of his feed store is not highly productive of information relating to any riddles and emergencies that may afflict the community. A heavy-set, agreeable man, he frankly states that the main function of the mayor seems to be to sign checks. In addi-

---

[1] The only Democratic candidate for sheriff who had a campaign plank was Everett Jarrett, a house painter. ("If I am elected, the jail will get a new coat of paint.") He ran ninth and last.

tion to this activity, Mr. Michel "works with the Chamber of Commerce and other civic organizations when they want my help." Recently he played an important part in the town's successful effort to induce the Ralston Purina Company, feed manufacturers, to set up a new plant in Vandalia to replace one that had burned down in East St. Louis. The mayor also feels that he ought to "check complaints that come in," but this is a full-time job, certainly not one to be discharged by someone whose feed business has a gross income larger than the town's entire annual general budget. The mayor also runs meetings of the City Council (he has never been an alderman himself, or held political office of any sort), attended by aldermen who are paid $20 per meeting. One such meeting recently authorized an aviation photography outfit in St. Louis to photograph land on Bear Creek, where Vandalia hopes to create a lake for a new water supply. The Kaskaskia River has become so polluted with factory-discharged chemicals that treatment by the town water-works is becoming prohibitively expensive. Another problem that has agitated the City Council was a degree of local indignation over stray dogs. In the absence of a definite policy on this matter, Marie Bennett, the city clerk, told irate telephoners that the best way to handle the mess was to lock up all dogs, homeless or not, until things blew over.

Michel admits that he ran for mayor because "they couldn't get anybody else." Such a basis of selection has been fairly traditional for many years. Nominations for political leadership are bestowed somewhat as they were in certain primitive societies, on persons who are the least skilful at evading the designation. Even lawyers have to be dragooned into running for court positions. An elective post in Vandalia is barren of power, of financial return, and of prospects for subsequent improvement. Given such a situation, the townspeople regard the biennial struggle to seize control of the Town Hall with only a faint display of emotion.

The columns of the *Leader* and the *Union* mirror the general unconcern with politics. Some of this editorial anaemia comes from a slightly stuffy sense of responsibility which dates back to when the Democratic *Leader* acquired the Republican opposition, the *Union*. Charles Mills, the tall, white-haired editor of the two papers, and one of the most overworked men in town, says that "ever since the opposition was bought out, we have had to realize that when we say something unpleasant about someone, he has no other place to go. We have to present both sides of everything. We think we've got an obligation to promote good activities and criticize bad ones regardless of the politics."

Mills takes a detached view of local customs. He says that city elections are not supposed to be political. "People run on a non-partisan basis, but sometimes it shapes up political. Mr. Smith, the former mayor, didn't put enough Republicans to work on the streets, so a lot of Republicans supported the Democrat, Mr. Michel. Well, the mayor has done pretty well as far as taking care of Republicans; the Board of Aldermen is Republican, too. Also, the county government is divided. We've had Democratic county officers and Republican Boards of Supervisors, then we've turned right around and had Republican officers with Democratic supervisors. The size of election pluralities varies from around 1,500 in favor of the Republicans to 1,500 in favor of the Democrats. There's a lot of personality voting. We've got our radicals and our rabids, but people as a whole are more interested in the best man for the job, and, as far as the papers go, we don't like to do too much endorsing of candidates and lacing them up and down in elections. We have to work with everybody, and if a man we oppose gets elected, we have to remember that we have to do business with him. We have to work with him for four years. I don't mean that we're afraid of criticizing the administration. We're doing it right now."

Such philosophizing doesn't sit well with some of the town's old-time Democrats. One of them, reporting that Democratic county advertising helped the *Leader* stay alive during the hard days of the depression, says, "Charlie Mills got less Democratic as soon as he got the wrinkles out of his belly." Whatever the situation may be, the GOP still has a spokesman in the *Union,* which as far back as April, 1959, ran up its colors by calling for the election of Republican candidates everywhere.

The other customary sources of small-town disturbances and civic strife are also unpromisingly dry. "People behave pretty well here, considering," says Robert Burnside, a local lawyer who would know better than anyone who was misbehaving, since he defends a large number of them in court.

This is not to say that Vandalia conversation is totally deprived of juicy subject-matter. Last winter the *Leader* printed the details of the foiling, through a tip to the police, of a young man's attempt to stick up a local supermarket; and any citizen, asked to recall examples of irregular or anti-social behavior, will recount the story of two cases of prostitution nipped in the bud by town constables. But, except for a brief flurry of store robberies, a two-man police car has been able to keep Vandalia law-abiding at night. A first impression that Vandalia is unpolluted is confirmed by more detailed investigation.

Its respectability and churchliness do not set Vandalia apart. Most of its neighboring communities, heavily populated by German Lutherans, Baptists, and Methodists, are relatively free from dissension or violence. Whether this is the result of an abundance of Christian virtues, good police work, or simply an elaborate system of civilian intelligence work is not clear. What is clear is that it is impossible to be in Vandalia very long without being noticed. Vandalia's social and moral regularity depends greatly on several thousand pairs of eyes. There is nothing malicious or prying about this sort of surveillance. In a small town one does not peep, one sees, whether one wishes to see or not. When a housewife goes to market, she learns where she has been soon afterwards from an interested friend. Ministers have come to rely heavily on kind-hearted parishioners for information on what members of their flock lie ill at home or in the hospital. In a town where the lives of their neighbors are the yarn of everyone's knitting, it is possible to be immoral, but utterly past imagination that one remain undetected. "It's positively neolithic how things get around here, positively tribal," exclaims a recent arrival from Europe who, it should be added, lives in Vandalia because he likes it.

This kind of atmosphere is a mixed blessing. While many Vandalians appreciate the neighborly sort of mutual assistance in an emergency which is a standard fact of life in a small town, there is also some feeling that sympathy and first aid from one's fellow-citizens are often bought rather dearly—at the sacrifice of individual privacy, for instance. "Nobody could ever die in Vandalia and not be missed right away," says one complainer, "but sometimes I think I'd prefer a big city. At least you can live without being noticed, even if you may decay in your apartment for several days after you're dead." The almost familial social climate also tends to create an illusory sense of security and complacency. The Presbyterian minister, a pipe-smoking transplant from Cincinnati named Ralph Smith, has preached more than one sermon on "Peaceful Valley" in the hope of stirring up a little healthy discontent, without noticeable success. "This is a fine community," he says sadly, "but I sometimes wonder if we aren't just an island of the past floating into the present."

One ancient pattern of behavior at which Mr. Smith, almost alone among his fellow-ministers, has publicly aimed his irony has been Vandalia's treatment of the Negro. "We call our town the land of Lincoln [2] but the hotels won't rent a room to a Negro, and no Negro can buy property or rent a home in Vandalia. There is an old saying that people in Vandalia are glad to help a Negro as long as he keeps on going right out of town."

There is some improvement taking place in the situation, he notes. Charles Truitt's Abe Lincoln Motel on St. Louis Avenue and the Riviera Motel on Route 40 take Negroes, and they have been seen eating at the Abe Lincoln Café and the Patio Restaurant. But with the exception of Mr. Smith and a handful of others, the town's anti-Negro habit patterns have not bobbed to the surface in public conversation.

The reluctance of the town's churchmen to take up the matter was demonstrated this year in the period designated nationally as both Race Relations Week and Boy Scout Week. While Mr. Smith made the day an occasion to remind his congregation of Vandalia's "color-blindness" and to read the lesson of the Good Samaritan, the topic was not belabored in other pulpits. The printed program of the St. James Lutheran Church informed its readers of Boy Scout Sunday but refrained from mentioning the other designation.

It would be unfair to Vandalia, however, to ignore the

---

[2] Local antiquarians have mixed feelings about Mr. Lincoln, who was largely responsible for moving the state capital from Vandalia to Springfield.

fact that the town's treatment of the Negro has occasioned a great deal of subterranean soul-searching. With the prospect of the township's only Negro pupil coming to Central Junior High next year, the Board of Education has discussed the problem of how to bring about this first experiment in integration successfully; and the teachers at Central and their principal have quietly determined that it shall work. Two years ago Vandalia's park commissioners, asked for a policy decision by the Superintendent of Parks, voted unanimously to operate the town's swimming pool on an integrated basis. There have been some interesting educational efforts with the community's young people, too. Spirited discussions on integration have taken place in some high school classes, perhaps precipitated by Mr. Smith's baccalaureate address last year on the subject. Although it may be that future tests of Vandalia's traditional attitude toward the Negro will provoke bitterness and controversy, it is probable that the issue will be resolved intelligently and fairly in the end. Intelligently, that is, if the most influential people in the community assert their leadership. Almost without exception, the educational, religious, and professional leaders of the community acknowledge the injustice of the old attitudes.

No conversation with these same leaders proceeds very far before the same set of worries rises to the surface. Details and emphasis change from person to person, but the discussions stress related difficulties: scarcity of jobs, lack of town leadership, the shortage of good housing, and the growing problems of the school system. The problem at the root of all the others is the economic decline of the entire county of which Vandalia is the center. The shrinking of the farm population has made is clear that Vandalia will have to rebuild the basis of its existence. There is nothing particularly altruistic about the worries over the disappearance of the farmer. What will happen to Vandalia when the county becomes a largely de-populated assortment of land-holdings in the control of a few operators is a decidedly unpleasant question which troubles both the old-timers and the relative newcomers. The town cannot expect to maintain even the nearly im-perceptible population increase of the past unless new cus-tomers replace the farmers who go away, or unless some other sort of occupation presents itself to the people who used to cultivate the small farms. One thing is certain: no matter what direction Vandalia's development takes, the rural style of life is slowly passing and with it the tranquil-ity of the community that has always been the core of this farming area.

Although the local government is inadequate to give the town leadership in solving its economic problems, there have been some instances where the enterprise of a few in-dividuals, backed by the townspeople, has had a marked effect on the town's fortunes. When banker Rogier was president of the Chamber of Commerce, the organization was able to win the support of the townspeople in an ef-fort to attract several small industries. A shoe manufactur-ing company, Johnson, Stephens and Shinkle, had occupied for many years a brick building on the west side of town. In 1957 the company shocked everyone by announcing that the plant was no longer adequate, and that the company was thinking of moving elsewhere. The Chamber of Com-merce assured the company that it would try to raise $75,000 to help it build a new plant. The drive netted $77,000 with the largest contributions coming from the two banks, with $2,500 each, and from the American Le-gion, which gave $2,000. Members of the Boot and Shoe Workers Union (AFL-CIO) working at the factory contributed $12,000 out of their own paychecks.

"Everyone who had a job in town was asked to give, and almost everyone did," recollects Rogier. "Of course, this was the sort of thing you aren't supposed to do—subsidize an industry to keep it around, but we did it because it was either that or lose the plant and all the jobs that went with it. We made an outright gift of the money to the company. There were no strings attached. As a result we kept the largest single industrial employer the town has ever had."

This was one chapter of the town's effort to protect its economic future. Another chapter soon followed. The old shoe factory remained vacant for a few years but finally the Chamber of Commerce decided to try to find a tenant. It bought the building from the shoe company for $28,000 and modernized it, with a $68,000 loan from the Small Business Administration. Then the Chamber's Civic Advancement Committee went to the townspeople for the rest of the necessary capital. Again the drive was successful, the people giving $32,000. The new occupant, United Wood Heel, which had done a great deal of business with Johnson, Stephens and Shinkle, moved in. This time no gift was involved. Over a period of years the townspeople's contribution and the SBA loan will be paid back by United Wood Heel in the form of monthly plant rentals.

A third industry, the Princess Peggy dress company, was also obtained as a result of Chamber-inspired activity. "In 1949," Rogier reports, "when we hadn't had a new industry in here for some time, we got some indication from the Singer Sewing Machine Company that a garment industry could be persuaded to locate here. We told them we'd provide a building, and we raised $107,000 to do it. Princess Peggy moved in with a long-term lease, and they pay only upkeep and insurance. There is no rent. The Chamber's Civic Advancement Committee stills owns the building, but in a practical sense the $107,000 was an outright gift from the people of Vandalia."

Although the town's fourth and most stable and expanding industry, the Crane Packing Company, manufacturers of mechanical seals, came in on its own without subsidy of any kind, the town's initiative at an earlier date made this acquisition possible too. In 1954, the Chamber persuaded an outboard motor company to move to Vandalia with the promise that it would give the company land alongside the railroad tracks plus $31,000 from the town, contingent on the company's meeting certain payroll requirements. The factory was built and the company moved in, but it failed. Four years later the availability of the plant helped attract the Crane Company, which bought it.

These negotiations and the unusual response of the townspeople are generally regarded in town as a demonstration of how far Vandalia can go with energetic leadership able to explain itself to the public. It is also an illustration of how essential such private leadership is to Vandalia's future.

Evidence, therefore, that the town is having difficulty finding a new generation of leaders to replace the old ones has disturbed many Vandalians. Rogier is depressed by the fact that the town has not developed an effective local government to cope with the growing needs of the community. With all our talk about the responsibility of local government, he points out, the fact is that we have practically no local government whatsoever. It is just this sort of situation which results in the state and federal government coming more and more into the picture. The town's fiscal policy leaves something to be desired. Despite its many obvious needs, the town has never issued bonds, except school bonds, and, without such indebtedness, Vandalia is unable to avail itself of various types of federal assistance. "Whether we like it or not, lack of a debt is regarded as a sign of a lack of effort of the local community to meet some of its own problems. Nearby towns like Taylorville and Shelbyville have demonstrated that they are making the effort locally, and as a result they have gotten federal help. We have also suffered from a lack of town planning. It hasn't been until just a little while ago that we set up a city planning and zoning board. Lack of planning is one of the big reasons why Vandalia has not grown as it should."

It would be pleasant to report Vandalia's factory drives had turned out to the perfect satisfaction of everyone concerned. Such, naturally, was not the case. One local clergyman bitterly points out that the fund drive was the first demonstration, repeated since, that the town's wealthiest citizens were "way down in a low bracket of coming across —the ones that had the money held back." [3] There is little question that Vandalia's industries have given the town some measure of economic relief, but, with the exception of the Crane Company, they have also contributed to a nagging sense of community insecurity. The shoe and heel industries, acquired at such expense of money and energy, often hint, when wage contracts are to be negotiated, that departure to other areas known for low wages is a possibility. Other intelligence in the form of circulars, distributed to employees at contract time, describes the company's operating losses and is distinctly unsettling. It is well known that the shoe and heel companies operate rented equipment and would have less difficulty moving away for this

---

[3] There is considerable testimony that the town's wealthier citizens are ungenerous contributors. Even the children have noted the phenomenon. After a UNICEF "trick or treat" campaign, nine-year-old canvasser Randy Parker reported that "the poor people gave us half-dollars and the rich people gave us dimes and nickels." Another drive chairman, Mrs. Maurice Shulman, says, "When we have a campaign, many of our wealthier people— the so-called leaders—give practically nothing."

reason than a company with heavy investment in production machinery.

The insecurity engendered by what information the companies choose to give out has severed the spine of the factory employees' unions. The consequence is a firm ceiling on hourly wage rates starting at the legal minimum of $1.15 per hour and ending around $2.25 for piece workers.

IF anyone has learned to live with the hard facts of an unremunerative occupation, it is possibly Clifford Tedrick, the slight, smiling, fifty-nine-year-old financial agent of the Boot and Shoe Workers Union local at Johnson, Stephens and Shinkle. He has been a piece worker in the factory for thirty-five years, and his take-home pay amounts to slightly more than $60 a week. He is as far from embitterment as a man can be, but he speaks of his situation sometimes in a slight tone of disbelief. On his own earnings and those of his wife, he has raised a family, owns a neat red brick house on West Edward Street, a boat, and a red Chevrolet.

It was for the privilege of continuing to be employed for $1.15 to $2.25 an hour that Tedrick and his fellow employees gave $4.00 a week from their paychecks until they had donated $12,000 to their employers for a new plant. He smiles wryly at this. "If we hadn't raised the money to keep the factory here, some other town would have gotten it." And it is the continued prospect of "some other town" anxious to lure the shoe company away that makes it almost impossible for Tedrick's union to negotiate with management with any real bargaining power.

Tedrick is a mild-mannered man, not inclined to gripe or blame anyone for his or his fellow employees' predicament. A portion of whatever dissatisfaction he feels seems to be directed at the national labor movement as much as at the dismal economics of the shoe business. Every union is out for itself, regardless of what happens to other people in the movement, he says. "It's hard on a man who earns a couple of dollars an hour to pay a plumber or a carpenter or an electrician three or four times as much to work on his place. A pound of butter costs me just as much as it does a carpenter. Union people aren't treated equally by the union movement. The big unions ought to do something for the lower-paid workers instead of pushing up the wages that are already way up there. Take the steel workers. I'm for everybody getting a good wage, but I'm not for some people getting everything and others getting nothing. Every time the steel workers get an increase, we have to help pay for it."

Tedrick was responsible for one dramatic display of the unsolidarity of the local labor movement. At a union meeting called to hear union barbers protest that shoe workers were not patronizing the organized hair-cutting establishments, Tedrick demanded that the afflicted barbers remove their shoes and display the union labels. The barbers indignantly refused to comply.

A long time ago, when the limits of his hopes began to dawn on him, Tedrick had thought about leaving Vandalia. "I might have gone at one time, not now. This house is my home. It's not much of a place, but it's a place to stay." He has been putting in some new floors, and remodeling some of the rooms. "My wife is head nurse at the hospital annex, on the 3 to 11 p.m. shift, five days a week. My boys are grown up now and work for the Wabash Railroad. My daughter and her husband work for the Crane Company. I don't want to leave Vandalia now. One thing you can say about this place is that people look out for each other here. People will help if things go wrong."

A less philosophical view of the local economic situation

is taken by James Harre, who heads Local 1048 of the
Common Laborers' Union (AFL-CIO), with a membership of 150 unskilled and semi-skilled workers. They handle
jobs ranging from "dirt shoveling" to laying of oil pipe-
lines, with wages running from $2.30 to $3.20 per hour.
Some of Harre's members are farmers who work part time
on highway and carrying jobs. He is an outspoken critic of
the local Chamber of Commerce, declaring that far from
displaying energy in its efforts to attract industry, it has
not followed through enough. Vandalia is gradually going
downhill, he says, because people are having to go out of
town or move away to get factory work—sometimes to Effingham at the Norge plant, or to the Caterpillar plant at
Decatur.

Harre thinks the town could have had the Caterpillar
plant "if anybody had really worked hard on the company.
The Chamber doesn't want big industry in here because it
would push wages up, and it doesn't want them up. If we
had more industry there would be more money in circulation. The stores could afford to pay their help more. I don't
care about big defense plants coming in, but we have to
have more industries, ones that are stable, that make farm
machinery and clothing, not war machinery. We are in
an ideal spot for industry, but we're not doing much about
it." Expression of a viewpoint like Harre's is generally considered unpatriotic in town, but there are a number of
Vandalians who have similar feelings.

One Vandalian who does not hesitate to express some
rather sour views on the state of affairs is Father Francis
Gribbin, pastor of the Roman Catholic Mother of Dolors
Church. Father Gribbin is a tall, slightly bent Irishman,
with penetrating blue eyes and a well-concealed sense of
humor. From his various observation posts he has concluded that Vandalia is less than a progressive community.

"There are a lot of people in this town who are not enthu-
siastic about what would be a decent living wage for people," he declares. He watches local families as they shop in
the grocery stores. "Fellows with three or four children
go in. They buy the staple goods and only that. There are
no candies or cookies. That's out. I've seen mothers of large
families who will come in on a Saturday evening and buy a
pound and a half of hamburger for their week's supply."
Father Gribbin pauses, then, more intently: "What's needed in this town is a little more buying power."

Only a handful of the factory workers are members of
Father Gribbin's parish. His indignation spills out over
any sectarian boundaries. "Man is a human being and he
has a right to be treated like one. If there is one man
who is ill-treated in your town, you can be ill treated, too.
As long as one man is kept from his freedom, your life
is in danger. As long as one man is a slave, you can be a
slave, too."

In the face of its declining economy, Vandalia can ill
afford to undergo another misfortune—the loss of many of
the young people who might have provided a new generation of leadership to the town. Youngsters with an ambi-
tion to earn a respectable living and raise a family of their
own cannot picture a future for themselves in Vandalia
no matter how much they may like it. The future for a
young person in Vandalia, measured against the attractions
of the city in terms of high-paying jobs, the chance to specialize in a profession, and the availability of culture and
entertainment not provided at home, is what lies behind
the attitude of one of the high school's brightest graduates
of a year ago. "Even though it's considered fashionable to
knock Vandalia as a dead place, I'll always have a sort of
adoration for this town," says a University of Illinois fresh-
man named Mike Waltz, who graduated second from the

A VANDALIA PORTFOLIO

AN ABANDONED FARM *"We have had a revolution in this country, a revolution in agriculture. When we lose a farm family, the banks and the retail stores lose a whole family of customers. Other groups, union and management, can set their prices and operate under some reasonable assumptions. And when they set their prices, they don't have to worry about how it affects anybody but themselves. But some farmers can't ever know their prices in advance. So there he is, a seller in a buyer's market, and a buyer in a seller's market when it comes to farm implements."*

CHARLES EVANS *"We've never had a setback. We've never had a boom. A big percentage of people own their own homes. This makes us a good town for a factory. We have good, sound, sincere bankers. I think the town is going to develop pretty well. I don't know what we're going to have to do to keep our young people here, though. When they go to the city, they don't come back."*

HAGARSTOWN RURAL SCHOOL *Rural attendance centers are still a source of controversy between the farmers and the townspeople, but the argument soon will be an academic one. The six that are left of the township's original three dozen one-room schoolhouses are expected to disappear as the teachers in them retire or leave the system: there will be no teachers to take their place.*

"The school system ought to get youngsters to think for themselves, learn how to figure things out. We need highly skilled people more than ever, men who can accept responsibility. The answers aren't lying around. They have to be invented."

REV. RALPH SMITH *"The church has ceased to be the center of social activity in this community. I sometimes wonder if we aren't just an island of the past floating into the present. People here don't see the world outside Vandalia as having anything to do with them. This is a very quiet, stable community. The drugstores sell a lot of tranquilizers."*

ALENIA MC CORD *"We have our standards and tend to be a little intolerant of other people if they don't agree with us, but we don't try to railroad our standards on others. If somebody doesn't come up to our standards, that's all right just as long as they keep a long distance away from us.*

"We don't have even one real bookstore in Southern Illinois, but this doesn't mean that people in town don't read and that our students don't read. One of the problems is that many of the youngsters don't have too much time. Youngsters are more interested in making money than in anything else. That's what you can expect from our society, where you have an emphasis on what is good for YOU, *what you can get out of it, rather than what you can do for other people."*

LEO MURRAY "My big problem is finding land to rent. It's so scarce you almost have to buy these days, and this means fifty or sixty thousand dollars for a decent-sized farm. I can look around at farmers who don't know from one year to the next when their leased land will be sold out from under them to someone —very often someone who isn't a farmer."

IVAN SNYDER "Farming is nothing but a big business now. You starve to death on eighty acres—even on twice that much. The boys want to be farmers, and I've tried to talk them out of it. This is a hard thing for me to do, to tell my oldest son he can't do the thing I wanted to do when I was his age. What should I do—tell him to look for another kind of job he can't do as well, a job that doesn't even exist?"

GALLATIN STREET *"It's positively neolithic how things get around here, positively tribal. Nobody could ever die in Vandalia and not be missed right away, but sometimes I think I'd prefer a big city. At least you can live without being noticed, even if you decay in your apartment for days after you're dead."*

top of his high school class last year, "but I guess from now on I'll never be more than a visitor to Vandalia." There is little the father of such a boy can or wants to say to bring his son home again.

The situation, of course, is even more difficult for the children who do not go on to college. They now are forced to go to Chicago, St. Louis, Indianapolis, or Decatur, where there are semi-skilled or skilled factory jobs. Almost every farmer has sons and daughters who have gone away to live in apartment houses, go to work in a car pool, and receive economic benefits as foreign to their fathers and mothers as Russian socialism. It is inevitable that the son who belongs to the United Auto Workers local at a Ford Assembly plant in Chicago will have some effect on parental thinking: the farmer speaks of labor unions today with a sense of frustration and bewilderment, but the old angry tones are often missing.

For a community that has always tried to handle its own problems the choking-off of its source of community leadership is alarming. Vandalia's slow advance has depended largely on the energies of a few private citizens with some ability to sense the future and organize civic efforts. The dependence on these private citizens has been especially great because of the town's lack of any real tradition of political self-government. It has been the Chamber of Commerce, not the Town Hall, that has instigated most of the programs designed to advance the town's interest. It has been a handful of wealthy, often rather paternally minded businessmen, rather than town boards or commissions, who have had the ideas and given money for the community parks and the library.

The hope that future leadership could be obtained from young professional people has not been realized. The present members of the bar association are not, with occasional exceptions, participating actively in local town government. Most of them are involved in practices so demanding that they have neither the time nor the energy to make a consistent contribution to dealing with the problems of the community's future. This is even more true of the half-a-dozen doctors, who are overworked and unreceptive to the idea of participating in local government affairs.

THE problem of town leadership can always start a debate between the partners of the town's most successful law firm, Robert Burnside, Democrat, and Joseph Dees, Republican, and in the course of one such discussion almost every worry and hope about the town's future bobs to the surface. Nearing fifty, Burnside is stocky, relaxed, with a mild southern accent that is typically Vandalian. Dees, several years younger, is a stand-up orator in contrast to his partner's easy-chair type of discourse. Very often the two men argue opposite sides of the same case in court, and they "tear each other up good," to use Dees's expression. They also have conflicting feelings about Vandalia.

Dees | "I couldn't ask for more out of my community. I like my political party. I've got a family that gets the right kind of education. I like the people here. We call each other by our first names. I like small-town life. I'm interested in people, and people are interested in us. As St. Paul said, we learn to weep when our neighbors weep, and enjoy when our neighbors enjoy. I wouldn't want to change. I'm active and have an active law practice. Even though we don't have the tensions and turmoils of some of the cities—maybe they are exciting—we've got variety in our work, and economically the town has been good to me. It's a different community. We're proud of the fact that it's different. We've never had any built-in corruption here.

We've never had a house of ill-fame, we've had no gambling problems. It's a clean town. The only time we ever had even any prospect of trouble was during the oil boom in the 30's.

"We have good churches. We have a good park and a swimming pool. We've got several new factories and we helped pay to bring them in. We've got a fine new hospital which is a tribute to any community, and an excellent new library which is a wonderful cultural center. Our Friends of the Library are doing a good job. They have arranged art exhibits; Mrs. Burnside, Bob's mother, is one of the exhibitors. This town is not dead intellectually.

"We do have our problems. We've got the problem of the young people who don't come back. I don't know how you solve this in a world of fast communications and specialization. You just can't specialize and live in a town like ours. We can't cope with all our problems. We recognize that we're going to lose a lot of our people because this is the sort of world we're in. If we want to stay in this town we've got to stick because we like the life and are willing to take the kind of pressures and the demands of unspecialization, of being a general practitioner, that a town like this makes on you. I'm not alarmed. We are trying to go ahead with the planning of our community. We're drawing up zoning plans. I don't think we're stagnant just because we live in a pleasant community. We can't be like the city, with all its advantages and none of its disadvantages, or a small town without its disadvantages. I'm willing to settle for what we have. But maybe that's because I'm a Republican."

Burnside | "I generally feel as you do, Joe, I wouldn't be here if I didn't like it. I like Vandalia better than any other town a hundred miles north or a hundred miles south. We have a lot of good, energetic people who have accomplished a lot in helping to build up this town. People like Charles Evans and Dr. Mark Greer, who gave the playground. But I'm a little pessimistic because I don't think we're going to have the leadership in the future that we've had in the past, and it's leadership that's always helped our town move. Good leaders, people who have had some vision, who've had some extra energy. Just in the last ten years I've seen a reduction in the number of independent enterprises. There are more chain stores, there are fewer people in business for themselves. The people who produced our parks and hospitals were independent professional and business men. If our young fellows go away to corporations to get jobs, where do we get the leaders? From chain stores and filling stations and ribbon counters?

"We've got trouble getting lawyers, not just our town, but other towns around here. We're the only town in the county that has lawyers, with one exception. We have trouble keeping doctors, too. There are four small towns in this county that have had to go out and subsidize doctors to get decent medical attention for their people. The trouble with the medical profession is specialization. You can't specialize and be a doctor in a town the size of Vandalia. We don't have the facilities, even with a good hospital like our own, which a specialist needs. So doctors steer clear of our town and other towns, which are worse off than we are because they don't have a hospital. Doctors can make more money in the city and they can specialize. This is true of the bar, too. Our bar association has shrunk by 20 or 30 per cent. My partner is the newest lawyer in Vandalia and yet he's been practicing here sixteen years.[4] Maybe we'll have to subsidize lawyers. This is serious not just

---

[4] A month after this discussion, Burnside and Dees acquired another member of the firm, Jack Johnson, a young University of Illinois law graduate who says he wants to live where he can be active in town affairs and where he "doesn't have to ride a train to work every day."

because we need lawyers, but if you don't have lawyers where are you going to get the people who have always been most active in civic affairs and politics?"

Dees | "A survey showed last year that the Fayette County Bar ranked very well economically with lawyers in other parts of the state, so it can't be economics that explains the lack of lawyers. It's specialization, just like the doctors. The old general practitioner doesn't seem to have the glamour that the specialist does now. Also, a lawyer in a small town, or a doctor, doesn't get the security and comfort with paid vacations and pensions and so on that he gets when he's working for a corporation. He's got to work all the time and his income is unstable—he may get $5,000 one year, $15,000 the next, and $10,000 the next. He dosen't get the vacations. I think the general practitioner of law or medicine has to take a lot more heat and gaff in a place like Vandalia."

A Republican who says he is not as pessimistic as Burnside or as optimistic as Dees is an ex-Naval officer, Martin Corbell, a serious-faced lawyer in his late forties who has lived in Vandalia fifteen years. "Our leadership is going to falter because we're losing too many of the best people. Many of the professional people educate their kids to the limit, and they are trained in fields where there are no openings in this area.

"There is one thing that will bring our young people back, at least some of them. It's the wholesomeness of life in this place. If I wanted to make money, I wouldn't stay in Vandalia. If I want culture and amusement, I can go to St. Louis to the opera, or the ball game, and I can get as good a seat as anybody else. Meanwhile, I can be somebody in my community. I don't care to be part of a big massive population blob so I can fight to be a lawyer in Chicago. How you are living, and what you do in life, depend on how you look at life, what your values are. If you appreciate the life of a small town, you'll be all right here.

"The fate of the small town is that it's going to become a satellite of some big community or city because of transportation and technological changes. The highways are bypassing us, and all the little communities around Vandalia are bypassed even by the farmers. They come to Vandalia to shop now. A small town doesn't have to die. It can just go to pieces, like Bingham, a little community near here. Once it was a lively place, now it's dead. On the other hand, there's St. Peter. This is a German prairie town, as we call it, an industrious community. It's a place that has good farms, good homes, good people. It had leadership, and that's the difference.

"One problem is that we have to recognize that the world is specialized, that we have to know our limitations. We've got to know when to call in the expert and the specialist, and not just assume we can do everything. But there's another problem in a small town like ours. It's not something you notice initially. After a while any young and vigorous man who is not a conformist, if he has a lot of new ideas and has achieved a certain amount of success, runs into trouble. Jealousies are created and pretty soon he tends to slow down. He tends to play it the way it is with everybody else. I don't like this—and it's something you find all around the country. There's too much of a conformist attitude about things. Nobody likes to ruffle the waters. Too many people are unwilling to stand up and say what they think. This is dangerous. It's why organized minorities are running the country. After the war we had a big membership in the American Legion Post here, and we'd get together and argue the merits of all kinds of things. I think there was better feeling in the community then than there has ever been since. But the discussions stopped. I hate to see apathy here. Maybe you should temper my judgment because I live in a world of conflict as a lawyer. Conflict is my business. Other people may get more upset by argument and discussion.[5]

"Also, there is a distinct habit among all the good-hearted groups here to ride a good horse to death. If a person volunteers for something and does a good job, then he never gets a chance to relax. Too many people are willing to ride him until he drops. If you look at the list of the contributors to the various drives, you'll find it's the same old civic work-horses that do the job and the same people who are always the free-loaders. The work-horses burn out and then drop away from community activities altogether.

"I spent a lot of time here as a volunteer fireman, and in the Boy Scout and other community drives. There isn't a phase of work I haven't been in. This is the way you have to begin life in Vandalia. The Navy was a help. It was a great leveler. I ran into all kinds of people. Yale men, Texans, hillbillies. It was a complex life. You learn to temper your attitudes about people. It helps when you come to a small town and run into the obstacles and butt your head. You run up against the establishment. Our Junior Chamber of Commerce found this out. But this is the way any group has to work. You have to get used to buckets of cold water being thrown on you."

VANDALIA has not been entirely unsuccessful in attracting young professional people. Six years

5 Vandalia's lawyers are unique in their community. A lunch table in the Abe Lincoln Café is the scene of peppery exchanges on all varieties of subjects. One week of noontime debates covered desegregation, the cold war, bureaucratic government, the policies of Alexander Hamilton, teaching machines, Supreme Court decisions, apportionment, the separation of powers, and Harvard.

ago Dr. Donald Rames, his wife Phyllis, and children (today there are four) arrived and bought a comfortable one-story brick house in the northern section of town. Dr. Rames is a physician who did not specialize. Another distinctive thing about him which impresses his neighbors is that he drives a Ford, not a Cadillac. The doctor, a tall, hefty redhead in his early thirties, and his equally tall and attractive wife did not have an easy time at first. She guesses that it took them about four years to "get assimilated."

Rames says that there is a need for general practitioners in small towns everywhere in the country. "The trouble comes from the sort of education a doctor gets. In medical schools the prestige of the specialist is pumped at you day after day. Specialize, specialize. In a town like this you can't limit your practice. Many doctors don't want to be in a town without a hospital. Too many medical students and interns want an eight-hour day. They want to live well. They don't want to have to work as hard. You talk to medical students and when they see your hours they say, I want the big city. We came here because we were small-town people. We knew what we wanted. But in medical school many of my classmates used to say they wouldn't know how to live in a small town.

"The trouble is that the hospitals in the cities are controlled lock, stock, and barrel by the specialists. It would be a wonderful idea to follow the procedure of the State of Texas in its medical schools, where during your junior and senior years you have preceptorships with GP's in smaller communities. Then you know what the situation is really like before you get out of school. This is what a doctor needs. It goes back to a well-rounded education. How can a medical student make up his mind what kind of practice really suits him best? He should have a taste of all kinds of practices. He ought to have a rotating intern-

ship where he'd spend three months on surgery, three
months on internal medicine, three months on obstetrics,
three months on pediatrics, and so on."

Mrs. Rames, who comes from a family of doctors, feels
that doctors have not been broad-minded enough. "They
specialize so much that they can only talk about isolated
parts of their own profession." She also thinks that the specialization of doctors is causing a growing feeling among
patients that doctors are "pretty cold people." [6] This impression is reinforced by the fact that a large number of
doctors pay little attention to the community they live in
and stick pretty close to their professional problems. "I
think more doctors ought to participate in things like the
Chamber of Commerce and other civic affairs."

If doctors are so preoccupied with their work and indif-
ferent to outside matters, does the American Medical Association really represent their views on such outside things,
particularly political issues? Dr. Rames thinks that in Illinois at least the doctors do keep in touch with their organized professional bodies. "We can be heard at the state
level. The Medical Association has offices throughout the
state where doctors can feed their complaints. Also, you
know, the AMA polls its members fairly frequently. It's
true that the average doctor is often too busy to be on
panels or write his district representative. But if he has
any complaints, he has only himself to blame."

Dr. Rames seems to be more interested in the American
Academy of General Practitioners. He describes their new
project MORE, which is trying to reverse the decrease in

---

[6] Vandalia exhibits widespread resentment against doctors as a group.
There is general irritation with rising medical costs and with the con-
spicuous affluence of most doctors in the area. There is also a frequently
stated belief that some members of the medical profession do not have as
much conscience as their fellow-citizens about paying their fair share of
the income tax.

applications to medical schools and the decline of people going into the medical profession. Why is there this decline? "Because the government and the people are glamorizing such things as physics, engineering, the applied sciences. For example, we had a Career Day at the High School at which members of the various professions met with interested students to talk about the possibilities in their particular fields. I had the smallest group of students."

"I can't remember one boy right now, except Superintendent Blythe's son, who is going to medical school from Vandalia," Mrs. Rames adds. "Medicine used to be a prestige profession, people used to venerate it, but the doctor's prestige is going down-hill. Maybe this is because he is beginning to speak up more and people don't like it. Or maybe it's because he specializes so much now that he doesn't develop a relationship with his patients any more. The general practitioner in a small town is looked on very differently from the specialist. He gets all sorts of wonderful letters and cards at Christmas and birthday times. That is one of the things that the specialist misses in the big city when he becomes one of a whole series of specialists that a patient goes to for some particular ailment. I think the general practitioners are the ones who are creating good-will for the medical profession."

"We know our patients pretty well in Vandalia," Dr. Rames says. "We mingle with them socially, we live next door to them. It is a good experience to treat a patient and see him get well. There are many specialists in a big city who don't have the slightest understanding of such a feeling. Of course, it's much more of an emotional experience for a doctor in a small town when things go wrong with a patient, too."

He reports that the younger doctors in town are stressing preventive medicine and pre-natal care. "Many of our patients can't figure out why their visits are so important while they're getting ready to have a child. We stress it. No matter how many patients I have in the office waiting for treatment, when my pre-natal cases come on their monthly visits, I see them right away. We have to educate people to preventive medicine. I know of cases in the past where the doctor delivering the baby didn't even know the mother's name, had never even seen her before. We're working up a series of lectures for expectant mothers. How to bathe a baby, how to exercise, and so forth."

Mrs. Rames says, "It's not just a matter of medicine. It's the security a mother feels in having someone looking out for her and her child all the way through the process. It gives it an importance. It's a matter of attention."

Last year Barbara Smith, wife of the Presbyterian minister, began going to Dr. Rames's colleague, Dr. Stanley Moore. Throughout her pregnancy she paid her monthly visits, and dutifully followed all directions, which included "stuffing myself with all sorts of vitamins." It was during these visits that Dr. Moore realized that they might have to prepare for a premature baby, and when it happened— the baby was born in its sixth month, weighing only two pounds ten ounces—everyone was ready. The struggle for life went on hour after hour for many weeks and each day saw the baby's slender chance grow brighter. Now Susie Smith weighs fourteen pounds and she is a healthy, happy child. It has been an important event in Vandalia.

III

Lawyer Martin Corbell's comments about the lack of culture in Vandalia are comparatively mild. A school teacher, repeating the views of most of her associates, says, "Let's face it, the place is a desert." The teacher is not exactly exaggerating. The local entertainment palace, the Liberty Theatre, exhibits only the most excruciatingly fourth-rate films, although distribution syndicates, rather than the Liberty's owner, Herman Tanner, may be the real culprit. The town does not have any concert series, theatrical groups, or local FM radio. Vandalians like Corbell can find the theatre, music, or a passable night club only in St. Louis, seventy miles away. The situation is, if anything, much worse for the teen-agers who have little chance to attend concerts or plays and a rather uneventful social life. High school athletic contests are one occasion on which the young people get together, although the usual Midwestern custom of dances after a basketball game does not seem to have caught on. The chief amusement spots are Nevinger's roller-skating rink and a bowling alley across from the high school. Those who want to dance have to go as far afield as Effingham to do it.

Some time ago, a group of high school seniors, frustrated at the lack of a social center, found themselves a small hall and proceeded to decorate it, with ideas of installing a juke box, Coke machine, and ping-pong table. But "Teen Town" collapsed when the minister of the First Baptist Church told the young people in his congregation to stay away. For the most part, the common substitute for something to do is for a gang to pile into a car and drive a traditional circuit in and about town, down Gallatin Street, around in the Kroger Parking lot, back up Gallatin, then out Route 51 to Route 40 to stop for a hamburger, then back on the raceway. Saturday night on Vandalia's main thoroughfare is a steady stream of flap-fendered vehicles, hot rods, and family sedans traveling in both directions and honking at familiar cars going in the opposite direction. The effect is weird in a town where, except for the taverns [1] and a couple of coffee shops, everything closes up tight early in the evening. "Where are they going?" one wonders. A young driver might answer, "Nowhere. But we're under way."

Some persistent souls have attempted to invigorate the town, not without resistance, but then again not without success. Many years ago, Anna Ruth Kains, an English and voice teacher at Vandalia High School, undertook a crusade on behalf of good music. She assembled a choral group. "We got together some nice high school girls—Catholics, Methodists, Pentacostals, and a Jewish girl, among others. We thought we'd offer our voices for Lent." The idea worked well for a while. Several congregations heard some well-trained singers, and the girls discovered something about the insides of churches other than their own. Before long, however, Mrs. Kains's efforts foundered on

---

[1] Vandalia's teen-agers stay out of the bars and prefer ice cream sodas at Cain's Drug Store.

the objection of a Lutheran pastor who wanted young
Lutheran ladies in his own church if they were going to
be in any church on Sunday.

Mrs. Kains had another go, this time at the formation
of a group to sing *The Messiah* during the Christmas
season. She was told by almost everyone that the town
wouldn't care much for that sort of thing, but she per-
sisted. A place to practice was not easy to find. One Methodist church turned Mrs. Kains down because the elders
had just installed a new red carpet and "they didn't want
the singers tracking it all up." But finally the Messiah was
presented at the Presbyterian Church and was a tremendous success. Later Messiahs drew so many listeners that
the audience spilled out into the street and onto the railroad bridge a few yards from the main entrance of the
church. So the Messiah moved to bigger quarters. It is now
presented on an improvised stage in the gymnasium of the
high school, which has no auditorium. The Messiah has become a Christmas institution.

Mrs. Kains also created a musical disturbance in the high
school. She asked the superintendent if the glee club, then
a rather sickly organization compared to the band, could
sing at graduation exercises. Previously graduation had
always been held in church, with choral offerings presented
by a church group. "After all, if we were going to have a
glee club, we had to have something to get ready for."
Permission was granted and the glee club has prospered.
Mrs. Kains related that in the beginning the band had
sixty-five members and the glee club seventeen, while now
glee club membership is up to 100 and the band has shriv-
eled to thirty or thirty-five. "Everybody in school who can
carry a tune has a chance to sing."

Significant cultural stirrings are also noticeable in the
public library donated last year by Charles Evans. A

Friends of the Library group has opened an art gallery in what had originally been designed as the Historical Society Room. The shows have been well attended, featuring the work of high and elementary school students, and some of the more practiced adults. This summer the library scheduled a traveling exhibit from New York City's Museum of Modern Art. Vandalians were well accustomed to abstractions by the time the show arrived, since a sizeable percentage of local art work leans to the non-objective. Some credit for this tendency should go to a young art teacher, Bob Barker, who teaches drawing and painting to nearly forty adults in evening classes at the high school.

The library itself has a store of 15,000 volumes, larger than most collections in many bigger and wealthier communities. The library compensates in part for the fact that Vandalia has no bookstore at all. The only local establishment that sells anything above the cheap paperback level is a local photographic supply house. In defense of Vandalia's reading habits, Mrs. Kitty Kelley, the librarian, reports that Vandalia's average circulation of six books a year per person is four or five times the national average.

The history of Mrs. Rames's efforts to organize the Friends of the Library in some ways parallels the tribulations of Mrs. Kains in her music crusade, both having been somewhat lonely campaigns. A graduate of the University of South Dakota, where she concentrated in literature, Phyllis Rames was determined not to abandon her interest despite the demands of a large family and her husband's medical practice. After considerable publicity, the first meeting of the Friends of the Library drew fifteen persons. Only three of these appeared for the next meeting. "I was just about ready to give up," Mrs. Rames declares, "but we did get some good suggestions, about holding a book fair and starting an art gallery in the library." A card party raised enough money for picture racks for the gallery. Arranging the book fair was like "pulling teeth." Mrs. Rames had to become the many-armed goddess of the whole affair. She "did" publicity, and apparently buttonholed everybody in the community. The fair raised $261, which was used to purchase an encyclopedia for the reading room. Last August Mrs. Rames could finally feel that her project was off the ground when 300 Vandalians attended an open house and signed up as Friends of the Library. This impressed the hitherto standoffish Board of Trustees of the Library. But even with a check for $100 from Coral Brooks, president of the Farmers and Merchants Trust, in her hand, Mrs. Rames is afraid to relax. "I'll have to keep pushing forever."

The community is scantily supplied with ladies like Mrs. Rames. The majority of Vandalian housewives, particularly the older women, are quite satisfied to play bridge and pinochle and chat about local matters. One active young woman, a new resident of Vandalia, says that after she had been in town for a while she was "horrified to find that most of my conversation with my husband turned out to be about what some people were saying about other people. We were never talking about books or ideas. So we made a resolution. We were going to cut out gossip, the way some people cut out smoking." Conversational paralysis in Vandalia is not always traceable to a predilection for card games. Television is also a major community preoccupation. However, while TV seems to have engendered a permanent adult fixation, Mrs. Kelley of the Library has hopes that the young people—more flexible and resourceful simply because they're young and not so habit-ridden—are returning to books. "TV pulled a lot of children away for a time. Circulation of books went down. Now the children are coming back to the library, especially in the

evenings. (The library is open for two hours every week-
day night.) Sometimes the place is really crammed full,
and evenings are just the time when the kids would ordinarily be looking at TV."

Whatever their opinions about the joys of reading, the
adults are quite willing to let Mrs. Kelley run the library.
Whatever complaints arise are usually about the $18,000
maintenance cost of the new building, triple that of the old
library, which saved money by siphoning heat from the
adjoining Town Hall. If the unlikely day comes when a
self-appointed book censor appears at the door, he will
find some difficulty in dealing with Mrs. Kelley, if past
skirmishes are any indication. A mother once slammed a
book down on the library desk—"it had something to do
with human reproduction," Mrs. Kelley recalls—and declared that if "anybody tells my child about such matters
it's going to be either me or my priest who does it." Nothing further came of the matter. Mrs. Kelley's postscript that
the lady has since left town only confirms the fact that the
troublemaker was a foolish woman to begin with.

Mrs. Kelley says, "Of course, we don't like pro-Com-
munist books, but that doesn't mean people shouldn't be
entitled to read about communism. They'll be more against
communism if they know something about it." Although
she calls various ministers and asks them for suggestions
about books for the library, she would not remove a book
from the shelves just because a minister wants it removed.
"Suppose someone objects to Paul Blanshard's *American
Freedom and Catholic Power*? Of course it wouldn't be
taken off. When you take one book off the shelf, when do
you stop?"

Despite the energetic efforts of such people as Mrs. Kains,
the Friends of the Library, the town's two librarians, some
local teachers, and a few others, it is doubtful if anything

but a major upheaval is going to improve the generally doleful character of Vandalia culture. There are some citizens who think a community college might do the trick, and that its establishment is a practical possibility. The college would play many roles. It would bring some higher education within reach of many high school graduates who, for academic or financial reasons, cannot go away to college but who could attend school and work part time while living at home. If, as has been suggested, the college provided training in vocational skills it might become a source of skilled labor that would attract industrial plants considering location in the Fayette County area. In addition, a college adult education program could stimulate whatever latent intellectual resources the town may have. The entry of a new teaching group into community life could make things more attractive to the town's professional people. The high school principal, William Wells, feels that the daily demonstration of a college program would not be lost upon high school students making their own plans for the future. Important people are interested. One, not surprisingly, is Harry Rogier. Others are members of the Board of Education, John Hegg, superintendent of the Crane plant, local ministers like Ralph Smith and Archie Brown. Charles Evans says he would "like to help." The nearby towns of Centralia and Effingham are talking about the community college idea, too. Vandalians don't like to take a back seat to anybody else, so they may just decide to do something about it. After all, Wells says, the town built three factories, why can't it build a college?

IV

. . . The United Nations and the Peace
Corps are fairly well thought of in Vandalia. Will Welker,
the nonagenarian lawyer who mows his own front lawn and
considers Hayes, Arthur, McKinley, and Cleveland the best
of the Presidents that have come along during his lifetime,
hopes the UN will keep on trying to find peace. John
Daniels is typical of many farmers who think the Peace
Corps is trying to do something important. But Welker
adds, "I've never heard anybody talk much about the UN,"
and last winter when the Peace Corps people tried to re-
cruit in Fayette County, nobody showed up. The town's
support of or resistance to policies set in Washington, except for the farm program, seems to be largely passive, and
the passivity frequently arouses the ire of some townspeople.

William Deems, administrator of the County Hospital,
says complacency is a "serious problem" not only in town
but in the whole area of Southern Illinois. "It's a matter
of economic complacency, among other things. Many
people ignore the fact that there are slums in this town.
Slums aren't hard to find. You just walk along the railroad

tracks through the backyards of any of our communities. I've lived in Baltimore, which at one time was supposed to have some of the most backward slums in the country. More outside toilets than any other city. I've seen children with their ears or noses bitten off by rats. Well, we have a very bad situation here too, and nobody is doing much about it.

"There is a good deal of divorce in the county. There are unwed mothers. We don't talk about Negroes. That's the trouble. There are no fingers pointed. We would raise hell with our neighbor if he let the grass grow too long next door, but if he needs help we don't really move the community in behind him. We ought to question ourselves as neighbors. There is no reason why there should be privation in this town. If you compare this town with a city, which is better off? At least in a city there are agencies to handle all the problems we face in a community like this. We don't have the agencies. We simply won't admit that the problems exist. We rely on a sort of good-heartedness which makes a person a public case for sympathy.

"What is needed in this town is a license to go ahead and find out how to do things that have to be done. The local government ought to be responsible for this. We should bring in the ministers. All the lawyers and other town leaders. People who share a common purpose are what makes a community. We should develop a plan and give it some official significance. Isn't it the responsibility of elected officials to point the finger at community needs?

"One example of stagnation is the lack of progress on our civil defense program. The program is vital to the hospital. A tremendous amount depends on our plans to handle mass casualties, and I don't necessarily mean from bombs. I mean victims of floods, fires, and tornadoes, which are not unexpected around here. If Vandalia could be accredited by the civil defense system we could get certain things from the government that the hospital and the town need badly. Fire-fighting equipment, for instance. Also we could have gotten $10,000 for a standby power generator at the hospital. Civil defense depends on local government doing something; it places the responsibility for acting in an emergency on the town officials. Yet we're doing nothing. I'm not just concerned about some nuclear holocaust, I'm concerned about the 'Spirit of St. Louis' coming down the tracks at 85 miles an hour. We will develop a hospital program for emergencies if we can get some leadership. Civil defense accreditation could have helped us with our ambulance service. Our ambulances are hearses run by private companies. If we could have equipped these ambulances with two-way radios, whenever there was an accident the drivers could let us know what to expect at the hospital. We could have paid for these with civil defense money."

ALTHOUGH the town has not responded very actively to civil defense, the subject is one of the few national issues, other than the farm program, that has provoked more than passing interest. A public meeting was organized last winter to hear an address by the executive director of the Illinois State Civil Defense Agency, Chauncey Carveth. Around 200 Vandalians, mostly men, including mayors of several nearby towns, the Superintendent of Schools, farmers, and local businessmen, gathered in the high school gym to listen and ask questions.

The problem of civil defense in Vandalia, Carveth said, was how to handle an estimated 50,000 people who would leave East St. Louis and move eastwards after a nuclear attack. Fayette County would be one of the receiving areas. Vandalia might have to function as an "island of survival. We might be completely cut off from east and west."

One of the first questioners was a young woman with a

neatly brushed page-boy bob.[1] She asked Carveth who was going to tend the 200-bed emergency hospitals if everybody had already gone underground for protection. Who would come out and get irradiated? Carveth replied that there would be a time lag of perhaps sixty minutes after the explosion of nuclear bombs in St. Louis and before fall-out descended on Vandalia. He also referred to the necessity for "harsh and cruel decisions" in such a situation, and the need for rescue teams and auxiliary nurses. Another question, about how Vandalia was going to take care of the refugees from an East St. Louis blast, seemed to unsettle the speaker. "I'll have to be like some Presidents we've had," he said, "and say, well, that's an iffy question." One of Carveth's associates rose to say that there is a plan that would distribute an average of one and one-half persons fleeing from the bombed areas to stay with one person from the surrounding areas. The speaker did not mention that, in view of the composition of East St. Louis's population, a high percentage of the refugees to be welcomed in Vandalia homes would be Negroes. A farmer then asked how radioactive air would affect the wells and ponds on the farms. Carveth suggested that every effort should be made to protect the water from dust.

The next questioner wanted to know what the Russians were doing about fall-out shelters. Carveth responded vigorously, "Shelters are all over the place in Russia. Do you remember those old root cellars we used to have back home? Well, ever since Americans started putting in frigidaires and deep freezes we've stopped building those good old-fashioned root cellars in the basement and the backyard. But the Russians, who don't have refrigerators, are still building those root cellars, and these are what they

---

[1] The same lady, appearing a few weeks later as a cheer-leader at a benefit basketball game, was identified as Mrs. Alice Walton.

are using as fall-out shelters. Why, I shudder when I hear one of my associates, who has been in Russia, telling of the tremendous construction of fall-out shelters over there." To the Russians fall-out shelters "are as fundamental as inside plumbing is over here."

Questions came back to the 200-bed hospitals. How much time would we have? Who would take care of the hospitals? Carveth plunged into a discussion of wind patterns, and warning systems functioning in Chicago and other metropolitan centers and estimated that fall-out traveling 76 miles per hour from St. Louis would arrive in Vandalia in about one hour. He concluded that if things really got extremely bad, everybody had "better button down for several days."

There was a final myriad of questions. How are we going to be notified if nobody is left in St. Louis to notify us? Who will give the information? How do we know when to come out of the shelters? How is anybody going to judge wind velocity? What about long distance telephone calls? How can we protect our animals? Carveth rose to the surface one last time to declare that the animals are going to have to take it on the chin just like the human beings. With that, one of Vandalia's rare public forums on national issues ended.

V

Even such a caustic commentator as Father Gribbin agrees that Vandalia's school system, despite some drawbacks, is a good one. The townspeople are particularly proud of the yellow, two-story high school on the edge of town, built in 1950. For the 500 students there are twenty-seven teachers, and the average class size is eighteen to twenty pupils, considerably less than the averages for the town's less modern elementary schools. With its gleaming corridors, bright, well-equipped classrooms, vast gymnasium, the high school is the most impressive building in the community. In the back of the high school a new one-story shop addition, built with a recent bond issue of $175,000, is nearing completion.

One might expect to find that the principal of the high school was an expansive, cheery man inclined to mellow comments about "what we are trying to do here." No such description would fit Bill Wells. He is slender, dark, bespectacled. He speaks quickly, with an air of preoccupation, and sometimes rubs his forehead in perplexity. He has been principal of the high school for eleven out of his twenty-one years in the Vandalia school system. Whatever satisfactions he may feel about his establishment are buried under his immediate concerns about the future of his students. It takes him little time to get across his points.

"Many pupils in the high school come from families with only a ninth or tenth grade education. Many of these are farm families. It's surprising how many of the parents never graduated from high school. The understanding of what an education means and what an educational system needs isn't something that comes easily to the people of our community. We have been lucky to have good leadership to help bring this about. We have to do things one at a time. We have to vote an addition to a school, then an appropriation for another school, then an appropriation for a shop.

"So far we have come along fairly well. But, believe me, we have problems. Our college-bound group is facing a much tougher life in college than they have in the past. Colleges are getting more difficult, the competition to get in is much greater. This means that at one end we have to give our students better preparation all the time. Yet we are not able to hold on to our best teachers. Good new teachers get a little training here and then they leave when they get an offer to go some place else where they can make anywhere from $500 to $2,500 more a year. We lose two or three of our best teachers every year to the nothern communities, the Chicago suburbs for instance.

"There is a great problem of how to finance our educational system here and it is getting worse. It is going to be tough in the next ten years. I think federal aid is so important. We've got to face the fact that in order to keep our teachers we've got to raise their salaries so that we don't have this great disparity with northern Illinois. And if we don't have these teachers, God help our college-bound kids. Can we keep getting another boost of money from the community? We're near the upper limit of our tax rate, which is fixed by law, and I don't know what we are going to do if we have to jump the tax rate—raise that tax limitation.[1]

"Our kids do keep going on to college. We've been able to put about 30 per cent of each class, even as high as 40 per cent last year, into higher education. This is a good record, particularly when so many families don't have a college background. The parents do encourage them, much of the time. We have real problems with the students who don't go to college, the ones who are going through the vocational program. We know what automation is doing. There are fewer and fewer jobs for ditch-diggers, farmers, and factory workers, people who do semi-skilled work. What happens to the children who drop out of our schools and who take the kind of vocational training that prepares them for jobs that are not going to exist much longer?

"It is a terribly difficult thing to be in a room with a boy who is trying to drop out, and you realize that depending on what you tell him a decision is going to be made which is going to affect his whole life, perhaps ruin his whole life. We try to convince him to stay, but unless we get help from the home it's very hard. Some parents just won't come in, partly because the boy himself is embarrassed by the parents, but partly because they don't want to talk to us. Sometimes the parents we want to talk to most aren't the ones who come to see us. It's just like it is in the elementary school PTA's. Very often the parents we see are not the parents that it is important for us to know.

"It's tragic to have to give up on a boy. Sometimes the students that I have been hardest on, have kept after most, who've been our marginal cases, our disciplinary cases, sometimes our drop-outs, have gone in the service, have worked, and then have come back after a year or two. Then

---

[1] So far Vandalia has not had to "anticipate" next year's budget to pay this year's operating costs, unlike neighboring high schools in such communities as Pana, Litchfield, Shelbyville, and Hillsboro.

they have become some of our good students. They haven't been a problem. Some of my best friends in the community today are ones who gave me the worst time when they were here during my days as a teacher and principal. I probably gave them the worst time that they've had, too. I've had drop-outs come back and ask me why did you let me do it, as if I had wanted to let them go. The kids are confused. They don't leave because they have to support their families, or they need money, so often. Sometimes they leave because of illness, but mostly it's lack of success, lack of feeling that they're accomplishing something which gives them the respect of the people they are with. Often they don't have any goals to shoot at.

"Then, of course, there is the automobile. A boy gets to be sixteen in this high school and he wants to get a car. It's the most damnable thing to face. That and going steady. The boy gets a part-time job so that he can pay for his car. There are no restrictions on it from many of the parents. The kid is out at night in a car, and school becomes a secondary matter. I can go right through the grade book and tell you the kids who have the cars. These are the kids we lose. We've had boys paying $55 or $60 regularly in installments on an automobile and buying their own clothes. They come in half dead in the morning. It's a status thing. It gives them a substitute for the success they don't get when they are not good students. One thing that might help reduce this feeling of failure in some of them is better grouping in our classes, but we're not big enough as a school to do this. I'd like to have more fast and slow classes. We try to do this in English and history and some of the required subjects, but we simply do not have the space, or the teachers, or really a big enough student body to justify this.

"We've tried an extensive athletic program as another

way of conferring some sort of status or feeling of success or identification with the school. The idea is that we want the school to be somehow the most important thing to all of these kids. We want to give them something that they can't get after school hours anywhere else. But the athletic program isn't working very well. We have seven interscholastic sports, but for some reason the interest isn't there the way it was a few years ago. I don't know why. Maybe it's because the kids are under great pressure. Athletics suffer from the competition with other things. We've only filled the gym twice in a long time for a basketball game. Our other sports are football, which is relatively new at the school, and wrestling, which is more and more popular. Then in the spring, baseball, track, golf, and tennis. I feel like a recreation director in the spring. Also, we have a chorus and a new band director, and we're trying to get a dance orchestra going. But I'm pessimistic. Half our student body has never attended one of the basketball games. We used to have a rip-roaring team and our players today are good boys. We don't have disciplinary or grade problems with them.

"We have a lot of trouble with complacency in the students. It seems to be one of the reasons why we have had such a poor academic class this year. But I understand that seniors in high schools all over the country are the same way. These were the students who were born a year or two after the war. How do you make them think? Well, the grown-ups have got to start thinking if they expect their children to."

No discussion with Wells can go on for very long. A bell will ring and he is on his way out of his office. An interview with George Blythe, the Superintendent of Schools, provides the information that a starting teacher with an A.B. gets $4,500 per year, while an M.A. starts at $4,800. After sixteen years' service a teacher can earn as much as $6,000. And that's about the top. A pension fund, to which the state and the teacher contribute, makes possible $3,000 annual retirement pay.[2]

Blythe is a heavy-set, middle-aged man with a pleasant manner. He says that the system is fortunate in having excellent leadership in its Board of Education, and reports that a year ago Vandalia graduates ranked the highest as a group at Southern Illinois University. Teen-age delinquency is not a problem to any great extent, he feels, because Vandalia is a stable community. It also has no social stratification to speak of—"the richest and poorest people play golf together at the country club"—and this has been reflected in the school. Blythe says that he is concerned at the drop-out problem and steady dating. "It wouldn't be so bad if these youngsters could drop out and work, but there are no jobs for them." He does not feel that there is any sense of cleavage between the students who are in the vocational program and those who are headed for college, because the high school is a small one and the students are much closer together than in, say, the New York City school system.

BLYTHE's and Wells' worries are shared by most of the teachers. A former County Superintendent of Schools, Lynn Price, now a physical education instructor, also thinks that the young people's interest lies outside school. "This is mainly because of cars. When a kid gets a car, his grades drop from A to B, or from D to flunking. A

[2] These salaries represent a recent raise of $200 per year. The high starting salaries as against the low salaries for experienced teachers is due to the desperate competition for first-year teachers. In relation to the lower cost of living in Vandalia, starting salaries are not too much less than the beginning figure of $5,300 in New York City, but the New York maximum is at least $3,000 higher than Vandalia's.

driver's license is to kids what being able to vote was for us in the 40's. Then there is the dating problem. By his junior year, unless he's pretty unusual, the boy has a steady girl friend. More often than not, owning a car and having a steady girl go together. The trouble is that so many parents want to give their kids more than they had. This leads to an over-permissive attitude. When a teacher tries to discipline a student, the parents' reaction is not 'what did my boy do?' but 'what did you do to my boy?' The business of handing the kid everything is one thing that gets him into a frame of mind where what he wants most is to be taken care of. He wants short-term security, and sometimes I think he would trade anything in the world for it."

A vocational training counselor, Doug Boggs, adds that the parents often spend a great deal of time telling the children to "go for security." Their attitude is "why work forty or fifty hours a week when you can go to work for a corporation thirty-five or forty hours a week, get better pay and pensions and other benefits. Too many parents are telling their children to specialize, that this is the way to make money. All of this talk makes some real problems for teachers."

One person who can be pinned down for more than a few minutes at a time is Alenia McCord, the high school librarian. She not only supervises the library but also teaches Latin. A small, engaging woman who has always lived in Vandalia, she has a greater sense of involvement with her community than some of the newer, younger teachers.

"We're not a wealthy community. Our farms aren't on the best land, but they're not on the worst. One of the most valuable things we have is our young people, many of whom have done very well in college. The only trouble is that most of our good academic students leave Vandalia and never come back. The ones who don't leave we try to give vocational training. It isn't easy for a small school to supply two sets of education." Aren't the students in the vocational program sensitive about being shunted into a different program from the college-bound students? "It wouldn't be realistic if there weren't divisions. The divisions have been there since the day they were born. But not the sort you mean. There is a great deal of overlapping in our two sets of education."

Miss McCord feels that the children are frequently more realistic about the direction they should take in their careers than the parents. "The children are very often pushed too hard because the parents have ambitions beyond the child's capabilities. The people value education. They've only turned down two bond issues, and this was because in both cases it would have meant sacrificing the rural schools, small, one-room counterparts of the little red schoolhouses of New England. These schools find it very difficult to get new teachers. The only teachers in them now are nearing retirement. When finally the last bond issue was passed it was because the farmers understood that the rural schools would not be abolished."

What about the students' reading habits? "We don't have even one real bookstore in Southern Illinois, but this doesn't mean that people in town don't read and that our students don't read. The students before seventeen don't go much for fiction but like science, history, stuff about horses, geography. They read much more than students in other towns around here. The school had to push hard to change the reading habits of the children, and lately the school has been trying to get more reading of the English and American classics. Once they get started, they love this type of reading. One of the problems about reading is that many of the youngsters don't have too much time after finishing their assigned reading. Many of them work after school, in filling stations and in stores, to earn money. Also, the farm children have chores, but this type of work no longer takes much of the youngsters' time. The reason is that most of the farms are mechanized today, so many of the country boys work in town now."

Miss McCord says that teachers from some of the larger schools up north, who visit the high school, say that they "have never seen children looking around for books and digging into them as much as they do in Vandalia. Of course, much depends on the particular student."

Is television cutting into the children's reading habits? Miss McCord's eyebrows go up in desperation. They still watch a lot, but she is happy to report that reading seems to be coming back. "The youngsters are getting tired of the same old programs, they're the same Westerns. The children would simply rather read. Another point is that the college-bound students get a lot of homework, and they simply can't do this homework and watch television. This has created some problems. Some parents object to heavy homework schedules for the children because they have to stay at home to help. This cuts down on their bridge and canasta. Parents, like everybody else, are getting so used to the forty-hour week that they feel that anything outside that forty hours should be completely free, and they feel, some of them, that having to stay home with children is a restriction on their freedom. This question of free time and leisure outside one's work is a hard one to cope with. If a child is going into a profession he has to realize that he doesn't have a week of twenty-five or forty or fifty hours, that he must be more or less on call all the time, that a profession knows no hours. Sometimes this is hard to get across to the children who are trying to decide whether to go into a profession or go to work in a factory."

In general, the youngsters are more interested in making money than in anything else, she says. "That's what you can expect from our society, where you have an emphasis on what is good for *you*, what you can get out of it, rather than what you can do for other people."

Miss McCord's views are remarkably like those of Mrs. Kelley, the town librarian, who says that young people are getting the attitude from their parents that the first thing one asks about a job is: "How much money can I make? It isn't a question of what I can do for anyone else, or whether I'll be doing work that is exciting or meaningful. It isn't what the boys want to be so much as why that bothers me."

How did Miss McCord get into teaching? She answered with a story about her little niece who had "verb trouble." When her niece was asked what she wanted to do when she grew up, she said she wanted to be a teacher "because we all teached." Miss McCord says, "That's the way a lot of us in Vandalia decide what we want to do."

The school system has had to depend heavily on teachers like Miss McCord who are native Vandalians or are married to men with professsional or business posts in the community. The new teachers who come to Vandalia are usually bad risks, because there are higher salaries elsewhere for them once they get experience, and because they simply become bored. Young, unmarried teachers find little companionship in a town where people of their generation either have not returned from college or have married very soon after graduation. Even if there were opportunities to meet single people their own age who shared some of their own interests, it is extremely difficult for the teachers to amuse themselves. "There isn't a night spot within thirty miles and if anybody caught us having a drink at a local tavern, we'd hear about it the next day from school offi-

cials." One group of teachers received a lecture after a
parent had reported that they had been laughing noisily
in a local restaurant. "We are expected to act like small,
grey mice," says one teacher. "We do."

To a young teacher, cultural prospects in Vandalia are
just as bleak as its social life. One bright young teacher
says he has no intention of staying because the town is not
growing intellectually. He blames this partly on the fact
that so many of its more alert young people move away.
"There are some well-informed people here, but there's
not much going on in a lot of people's heads. It's quite a
town for moral values, and it's a good place to raise children, but there isn't enough liberalism. People are too
close together. You get a feeling they're always peering
over your shoulder. No one speaks out on subjects. International problems might as well not exist. Who reads good
magazines and good newspapers? Not many. They don't
seem to have the time or want to make the time. It isn't
just Vandalia that's this way, it's all the towns in this part
of Southern Illinois. In a community like this a teacher
lives a pretty isolated life."

Some of the teachers admit that they are a rather in-
grown group themselves, that perhaps they exaggerate the
extent to which they are expected to conform. Townspeople have tried to draw young teachers into local activities with spotty success. Mrs. Rames, for instance, reports
that only a handful of teachers accepted invitations to the
Friends of the Library Open House, which drew a large
number of townspeople. And none of the teachers have
responded to Mrs. Charlotte Younger's general invitation
to join the Great Books program she is trying to start. A
young woman who is "frankly bored" in Vandalia questions her teaching colleagues' professed desires for intellectual stimulation. "What do teachers talk about when

they get together? Shop talk. There are never any very good discussions about politics and that sort of thing. Teachers talk about teachers, their classes, their teaching problems. They are the most self-centered people in the world." She reflects for a moment. "Well, maybe they are that way because they have to be. Who else gives a damn about what teachers think?"

VANDALIA's inability to offer its teachers salaries as high as in many other Illinois communities does not mean that it has tried to skimp on its educational system. It has given the schools good financial support most of the time. "The town does well by the schools," says Cecille Taylor, a young art teacher at Central Junior High. Her remark is significant because she is an outsider from Missouri, free from any compulsions of local civic pride, and because she is one of those teachers who are not returning.

The effect that the loss of an unusual teacher has on the school system of a small town is incalculable. Another person can always be found for the class, the same tests are given, but the whole school has a setback. "You don't get over losing them, you just accept it," says Central's principal, James Spencer. He remembers one teacher very well. "When I first came to town the teachers had never had regular meetings with the principal, so I suggested we might get together more often. The teachers suggested once a week. This was a surprise; I figured it wouldn't last very long because teachers never seem to have that kind of time to put into discussions. Anyway, I put another peg on the clock (so it would ring once more after the last class) and we agreed that any teachers who had to go could leave when the bell rang. The discussions went very well. We had a teacher named Floyd Collinsworth. He'd been born on the wrong side of the tracks, and he always had a very special interest in boys who didn't look as if they were going to get very far. One day he began to tell us about what excellent work one of his boys was doing. He described a theme he had written, which surprised everyone because we had never thought he had much promise. But Collinsworth went into great detail, quoting some of the sentences, and he told us how hard the boy had been working. At our very next meeting two teachers remarked that they had noticed that the boy was studying harder, and that his work was getting better." Spencer paused. "You know, nobody ever did see that theme Collinsworth was talking about. I don't think there ever was any such theme. It was a big help to one boy, though." What happened to Collinsworth? "Oh, well, we lost him. He was too good. He has a job somewhere in Michigan now."

One teacher who has stayed is Mrs. Irene Dieckmann. She teaches twenty-eight first, second, and third grade pupils in a one-room schoolhouse in Hagarstown, a few miles west of town. The school, a red building with an old belfry, built in 1897, stands a long distance back from the road in a muddy field with a few playground gadgets. Mrs. Dieckmann is a small woman in her early sixties with short greying hair, steel-rimmed glasses, and a face that manages to be stern and good-natured at the same time. She apologizes for the dirtiness of the classroom, saying that the janitor hasn't been in the night before and she has been trying to do some cleaning up herself. Some bright posters and drawings on the bulletin board brighten up a dilapidated room. "These are all made out of snowflakes," says Mrs. Dieckmann, pointing to some white paper cut-outs with very fancy designs. "We got quite a bang out of doing these. We all worked separately and then we all found that we had different snowflakes." There were also many paintings and drawings of Eskimos, who have a special appeal to the school children in this area, and are a standard subject of the art work. "In addition to brightening up the room, the art covers up the holes in the wall," Mrs. Dieckmann says.

She has taught in Hagarstown for seven years. She will be eligible to retire on a pension next year. This is unlikely. Mrs. Dieckmann is an active, confident person who would be bored doing nothing. She lives in Vandalia, drives out in a grey station wagon to the school, and has been teaching since 1921.

Mrs. Dieckmann's clothes, a brown cardigan sweater, white blouse, and a tweed skirt, fit the occasion. Cold drafts pour through cracks around the windows. "It's very hard to keep this classroom clean," Mrs. Dieckmann says, in a cheery, matter-of-fact way. "The wind blows through here at night something fierce, and in the morning there is dirt all over the place. We try to keep the walls painted, but they're so porous that paint won't stay on. I don't blame any of the new teachers for not coming out here."

The first grade sits on the left side of the room, the second grade to the right, and then in back, separated from the other groups by an aisle, is the third grade. Most of the desks are the standard schoolroom type, the seat attached to the desk with an iron bar, and the fliptop lid on the desk.

Class begins with the pledge of allegiance led by the largest boy in the class, who is wearing the standard dungarees and checked shirt. Most of the girls wear ski pants or just plain long pants, some of them in bright colors. When a class is ready for its recitation, it goes to a small table at the head of the classroom. While Mrs. Dieckmann is conducting the recitation, children from the other classes, who are supposed to be studying, come up at intervals and ask her to explain a word. This distraction seems to become more frequent when Mrs. Dieckmann is working with her fast group of second graders. In the middle of a burst of enthusiasm and discussion, a child from another class will come up and ask for attention, and at moments like this it is obviously difficult for the teacher to turn aside, even for a second. Somehow she manages, despite the interruptions, to keep the excitement going.

The first graders in their recitation quickly get into a lively discussion of dogs, of "boy dogs" and "girl dogs." There is a story about a "bad one that had to be tied up." Then there is another dog that fell asleep on a railroad track and the "train runned over it and everybody was just crying." Meanwhile, the third graders seem entirely absorbed in their books as well as most of the second graders, except for a few peekers and visitors to the pencil sharpener at the back of the room, a good place to observe everybody else in the class. Pencils seem to take at least fifteen or twenty seconds to grind to the exact sharpness desired.

The third graders have their recitation in the back of the room at their desks, this time in the form of a play about a magic horse, a doll, somebody named Molly, and an Uncle Robert. The reading has expressiveness, even glee, and is accompanied by some rudimentary acting, such as bows, curtsies, and movements of the arms. The children stand in a circle facing each other, a small theatre in the round. They read quickly and easily.

Shortly after the end of the play, Mrs. Myrtle Hopkins, who prepares the children's lunches in the basement, comes up to say something is leaking upstairs. Mrs. Dieckmann goes out back and fixes it. Later she goes down to the basement during a study period shortly before lunch to explain the lunch program (the basement has been converted into a little dining room and is filled with delicious smells of food prepared by Mrs. Hopkins). After several minutes, a couple of little girls come down the stairway to inform Mrs. Dieckmann it is time for her to be coming upstairs as everybody is ready for lunch. She looks at her watch and says, "Oh yes, it is," and goes back up. The children have washed their hands and are at their desks waiting.

After lunch Mrs. Dieckmann suggests that her visitor might like to take a picture of the schoolhouse. This idea interests the children who all feel it will be a good idea to be in the picture too. When the visitor drives off, the entire population of the Hagarstown School waves fare-well, with loud cries, and then begins scuttling about the playground for the few minutes left before school begins again.

RURAL attendance centers like the Hagarstown School are still a source of controversy between the farmers and the townspeople, but the argument will soon be an academic one. The six that are left of the town-ship's original three dozen one-room schoolhouses are ex-pected to disappear as the teachers in them retire or leave the system: there will be no teachers to take their place. A much more important, though less partisan, debate has been developing within the community over the nature of the high school curriculum, particularly its vocational training program. John Daniels, chairman of the Board of Education, and another Board member, Mrs. Maurice Shulman, share the principal's concern about high school drop-outs, and about the future of the young people who graduate from high school without any special skills. The high school has begun a program for some students who work in town during part of the day and attend classes the rest. Daniels reflects a considerable body of opinion in the town that feels the high school must do more to prepare

young people for a trade. Many of the graduates of the
high school, he says, might have gotten better jobs in the
big factories in Decatur and Effingham if they had had
trade school training. Yet he recognizes that at the same
time vocational programs may be outmoded rapidly by
automation. "What happens when these kids are trained
for jobs that disappear before they can get to them?"
Daniels concedes that a technical training program would
be inadequate, taken by itself. A vocational program would
have to be built on a base of engineering and science, so
that the student could adapt himself to changing technical
situations.

School authorities have sought advice on the vocational
program from executives of the Crane Packing Company,
among others. On its arrival in town, the company developed an on-the-job training program for its own employees which provided the core of its present production
work force. The school officials wanted to find out if there
was any way of relating the high school's program to the
future industrial needs of the county and the state. One
Crane official has views on the subject which were not what
the school officials expected to find.

John Hegg, a tall, rugged Chicagoan who grew up in a
machinist's family, is superintendent at Crane. He recalls
that his father would often bring home a product he had
made. "He'd show it to us and ask, 'What is it?' Then he
would talk about it, turn it in his hand, explain what it was
used for, why it was shaped the way it was. This is the way
you learn, not just about a single tool, or piece of
machinery. You learn the whole process of which the tool
is a part. The child gets a chance to listen and observe and
reason about the tool. This sort of exposure cannot be provided by any school.

"The family is one place where the boy gets the exposure.

The town he lives in is another place. There should be a demonstration going on all the time of the value of mechanical skills. There should be factories around where the boy can see the way this knowledge is put to work and what it produces. The trouble with a small town like Vandalia is that you don't have this surrounding demonstration. We have trouble finding people here with the sort of tradition that makes them suitable for work at the Crane Company. Farmers have some mechanical ability—something like what youngsters might get in a school course. They can identify a part and replace it or weld a break, but they don't know how to analyze a piece of metal and understand what its intention is, or what kind of instrument was used to give it a round shape.

"The problem is that we specialize before we have a knowledge of the whole. In the old days, a machinist was the master of an entire trade, but today we have only seventy-five or a hundred tool and die makers in the whole country, men who can go through the manufacturing process from beginning to end. The tool and die makers began at the bottom, sweeping floors. They ran everything—filing machines, grinding machines. They knew how to cut gears. They learned drilling, jig-boring, heat treating, and bench work. Now we have foremen who just supervise milling machines. Maybe they can do a better job on one thing, but they can handle only one job.

"Schools can't give a boy a future today just by teaching him a so-called trade. What they ought to give is basic knowledge. You can't put into a child what the father and mother put into him, and you can't generate the enthusiasm in the child that he gets in a live home situation."

When he talks about education, Hegg talks in terms of machine work because "it's my business. But what I say applies to any kind of schooling. A young man has to learn the functions of things and how to think about them. The outward shape, the day-to-day application of some particular piece of equipment, isn't important. The outward look of things changes—and if that's all a man understands, he'll be out of luck. A real machinist has to know how to grind, mill, sharpen, cut, and understand what is happening inside a piece of equipment. Even with automation a man like this will be needed. Mechanical processes are really thought processes. A good man will have to know the processes, even if he doesn't actually have to guide them every minute. Automation is bringing one very important change. We used to use a machine until it broke down. Now we have to know beforehand exactly at what points wear takes place and how fast, and how much it wears in relation to other points, so that we can prevent breakdowns. It's what we call preventive maintenance. This means we are going to need highly skilled people more than ever. We won't need button-pushers. We do need men who can accept responsibility. This is why the school system ought to get the youngsters to think for themselves, learn how to figure things out. So many kids have defeatist attitudes. They don't ever stop and thrash out something in their own heads. They have the attitude that the answers to every question are lying around somewhere and all they need is for somebody to point them out. The answers aren't lying around. They have to be invented."

Another Vandalian who has views on the educational program lives in a neat ranch house overlooking a lake on the north side of town. The manager of the local Illinois Bell Telephone office, Charles Younger, gives his opinion:

"If you teach a boy how to run a lathe, what good does that do if somebody eliminates the lathe? We have a terrible problem with people in the phone business who are filled up with specialized and obsolescent information, people who don't understand how to get at the theory of a problem. As soon as the little job they've been trained for is gone, they're unemployable. They become social problems. It's also difficult to re-educate them because what do you re-educate them for? Another job that is going to be abolished? The miners in West Frankfort, Illinois, are stuck because there's nothing they know except mining. They're in a community they can't leave and one in which they'll never have a chance to work again. As far as the telephone company is concerned, we just aren't satisfied any more with people who come in with some little technical trick they can perform. We want people who have degrees in electronics, people who understand the theory of radio engineering, not just wire splicers.

"Maybe there is a simple way of putting what I want a school to do for my children. Teach them how to question. The greatest sin of our educational system is that we just give kids information and then ask them to hand it back to us at exam time."

Mrs. Younger has her definition, too. "I think the idea of an education is to introduce a child to what is really alive in the world, not objects, but ideas and activity. We can do this through art, even through the use of their toys when they are young, and books. We should lead them to an investigation of life."

VI

: Although Vandalia may be suffer-
ing from other shortages, it is well supplied with churches.
A process of simple division reveals that there is one church
to every 400 people in town. The townspeople not only
join the town's thirteen churches but attend them regularly
and support them generously. Like other towns in the
"Bible Belt" of Southern Illinois, the churches have always
been at the center of the community's life. Therefore, it is
not surprising that Vandalia's clergymen should, as a group,
be articulate and informed commentators about their community. More than any other group they have accepted the
responsibility to be part of almost every phase of community life, and should they ever lose sight of this fact,
their parishioners are quick to remind them. On their part,
the ministers do not hesitate to lay about them a sharp
tongue whenever they feel a little castigation is appropriate.

Perhaps the most colorful minister in town is the Reverend Henry Allwardt,[1] pastor of the Holy Cross Lutheran
Church, with a membership of 300. He lives in a one-story
white frame house at some distance from his church, which
is north of town near the high school. A tall, bespectacled
man with a very thick shock of shining white hair, he works

[1] Mr. Allwardt died several weeks after this interview.

at a big oak desk covered with books and papers. After preaching in Ohio, Wisconsin, and Michigan and serving as a Navy chaplain in World War II, he came to Vandalia three years ago.

Mr. Allwardt begins with what is almost a standard opening to a Vandalian's conversation:

"There are several classes of people in the community. There are quite a few of the self-satisfied old-timers, a lot of them have good businesses and so forth, then there is a certain element, not as big as it is in some communities, of what I would call the decent, driven cattle. There is a kind of nice social life here, it's the best I've seen in a lot of ways. There is a certain amount of scandal, but on the whole things are pretty decent. I would rate it as a relatively pretty churchly town, not untypical of the communities in this area, and I've been around quite a bit. I haven't lived exactly in a locked trunk. I've been a pastor in the dead of the country, also in a big city like Detroit. A lot of people who behave very well in a small town like this fall away from the church when they get to the big city. It's not an entirely unprogressive community. The Chamber of Commerce has done good work getting plants here, for instance the heel factory. Vandalia is a lot better than the last place I was in, which was Arenzville. I also had a church in Marysville, Ohio. We had a 100-year-old church, and it seemed like most of the people in it must have been charter members."

What was wrong with Arenzville? "Why, everybody up there was so envious of everybody else. There was so darned much hatred. The stores would stay open even on Christmas for fear somebody else would sell something. The population was about 500. It was predominantly a German community. When you get into a German community you should understand the history of Germany if you want to understand the people; for instance, whether they come

from north or south Germany. Then you have to understand why their ancestors came to America. The people
in Arenzville came here because they thought they were going to get rich. Their standards were quite materialistic.
For instance, they didn't know a thing about baking cookies
on Christmas. You'd never find that going on in Arenzville.

"But take Vandalia. Look at my financial report, my list
of contributors. Here's a man who works in a shoe factory.
He has a daughter in school, and you know they don't earn
a lot of money in a shoe factory. His family gave $375 to
the church. Here's a truck driver with three children. His
truck has needed a transmission for a long time. He can't
even back it up. He's given $370 this year. Here's a woman
who works an eight-hour day, a widow. She has another job
as well. She gave $79. A bartender, whose wife works, $289.
There's only one man in my congregation you could say
is above middle income. I think he gave around $1,300.
The sidewalk around the church was paid for by two
people. Here's a farmer who has had a lot of trouble. He's
been on the verge of going broke occasionally. He gave
$218.

"Now look at attendance. We have good attendance. I
have two services every Sunday, and out of a total church
membership of 300 our average daily attendance for the
two services runs—let's look at these successive weeks: 281,
218, 245, 253, 267, 262, 236, 254, 245, 268, and so forth.
Well, that's a pretty good record. And it isn't because
they've got such a great preacher either. You'd be surprised
to see the number of men in the congregation. Whole
families come to our church, not just the women. About
a fifty-fifty split between farmers and city people.

"I have a lot of Germans in my congregation. They came
to Vandalia for quite a different reason from the Arenzville
people. They came because the churches of Germany did

not allow decent Lutheran preaching. Our Lutherans were in constant trouble over there because the State was trying to foist all manner of practices on the church that they didn't agree with. The Germans in this area came for what the Pilgrims claim they came for. And, by the way, the Pilgrims came because they wanted to be the dominant church. They are the most intolerant people who ever came here. It's too bad the Plymouth rock didn't land on them instead of the other way around. Our people wanted separation of church and state. They wanted a church that could operate unhampered. One of the troubles with our synod, however, was that our people were rather timid. They came in here with a church that was relatively unknown west of the Alleghenies. They were also a foreign-language church, and they felt that they had to feel defensive about this. But in a hundred years, since we organized our synod, which was in 1847, we've gone from twenty to 4,000 congregations in this area. St. Louis has the largest seminary in the world. We're busy in other countries too. We have eighty-three radio stations in Japan.

"What's that about the social activities of the church? I've got you, I'm a jump ahead. You mean, what does the average layman expect of church and what does he do in church? Well, that gets me into one thing. Theology is getting to be sociology these days, which means that a lot of people when they get in the pulpit feel they should never say anything that could be understood. The only trouble with most churches is their pastors. The pulpit has departed so far from what it is here for it isn't even funny. Why do I want to go to church to listen to lectures on prohibition and world affairs? What business has a minister got talking about matters that 30 per cent of his congregation know a lot more about than he does? My responsibility to my congregation is to teach the word of God, and if I happen to have some screwball opinions I'll keep them to myself. That's why we have pastoral conferences, to get ourselves unscrewed, we pastors. Another responsibility I have is to live like a Christian gentleman, and I also have the responsibility to bring children into the church with some understanding of it. The church is not a social club.

"The trouble with a lot of churches is that the Catholic Church is good for people who want soul insurance and the Protestant Church spends most of its time adding a mellifluous odor to the prevailing winds. Pastors ought to mind their own business and stick to their own responsibilities. Another job of the minister is to comfort and help the sick. This is his duty. You go to such a person when you're needed. You may have an opening with a sick person that you may never have again to bring him into the church and an understanding of God.

"I try to instill in the young people the desire to 'seek ye the Kingdom of God in his righteousness.' In these unsettled times this is the job of the church. I think my young people have pretty good moral character. You can't know too easily what they're striving for. The boys especially, though, seem to be serious-minded. The girls don't seem to have anything to talk about but boys when they get into high school.

"You ask about material gain, whether that's what people want instead of helping the community. I'll give you a thousand dollars if you can find three people in any community who aren't looking for material gain. Everybody is after it. Everybody all the way up to the President. Everybody is after what he can get."[2]

---

[2] Maurice Shulman, a successful young head of an oil-drilling company, makes the comment: "In our business we pay lip-service to the idea that we don't like pressure groups, but we're split underneath on this. We are against lobbies, but we have lobbies. We all want to feather our nest. We say we have the interest of the country at heart, but we're all looking out for ourselves, one interest group balances another, and that's the way things get done."

Mr. Allwardt brings up the probability that there is going to be another drive to push the saloons out of Vandalia. "It would only drive them from the city out into the country, and in the city at least they are under restrictions as to where they can be located. My old friend Archie Brown, of the Baptist Church, is the ring-leader in the Ministerial Alliance on this anti-saloon business, but I'll wham into this hook, line, and sinker. I don't believe in getting into this sort of outside political activity. I preach the gospel. Let the gospel influence the people, and let the people do the job. I don't believe it's up to me to stick my neck out on every local problem. I want to see that my congregation attends church and comes to an understanding of Christ. Right here I've got a list of eight people that I plan to kick out of the church this year, for non-attendance. I don't want their money. I want them to come here to this church, then the question of money will take care of itself. If the person doesn't come for the love of Christ, I don't want his money. But many churches do. I know one church with a big congregation where whenever they have a deficit they go around and some fellow who never goes to church picks up the tab.

"My job is to influence people to the Christian way of life, then if they're influenced they'll go out and work in their daily life for the things that they should. Now you take this dirty-book campaign of the WCTU some time ago. They got after some of these books and some of the women came to me and wanted me to testify. This was a touchy situation, so I said I'd go to the City Council hearing. I got a copy of *Lady Chatterley's Lover* and read it through, and red-pencilled all the dirty things. I went through it sort of diagonally, you know, fast, in about three-quarters of an hour. Well, I was sitting there and the mayor said to me, well, what did I have to say. I said first you've got to ask if the stuff is sold here. I presented him a copy of the book. But then I asked, why didn't the ladies bring in some evidence? Apparently none of them had taken the trouble to read any of these books and bring them in. Not one other preacher showed up at that meeting, either. But I told the Council, we're not here to tell you what to do. This is the Council's problem. But in view of the *Ulysses* case you have to ask what can be done. If the Supreme Court lets these books go through without censorship, what can we do here to stop it? But this sort of activity is not what a minister should be doing. My job is to teach the gospel, and to try to influence the character of my congregation. I do not believe I have the responsibility of molding the character of anyone outside my congregation."

THE Reverend Stephen Phillips has not the explosive personality of Mr. Allwardt, nor does he have quite the same view of his responsibilities as a pastor. His First Methodist Church, a block north of the Pennsylvania Railroad tracks, is an odd-shaped brick building with pointed towers, steeply sloped roof, stained-glass windows. The cornerstone was laid in 1900 and its battlements are a turn-of-the-century *patisserie*. Mr. Phillips is forty-three years old and has lived in Vandalia three years. He is a graduate of Southern Illinois University and the Theological Seminary at Southern Methodist University in Dallas.

"I don't know whether we're a typical town in this county, but there seems to be a feeling that it's difficult for new families to be accepted. People seem to be satisfied with their town, perhaps a little too much. When a man's satisfied he's not inclined to do better. Judging from my experience with people in my own church, I find them reluctant to try something they have not done before. They've gotten set in their patterns, they're entrenched in

their habits. This seems to be a characteristic of the townspeople (I don't know about the farmers, because there
aren't too many of them in my parish). But it makes for a
bad situation in a church. People aren't opposed to my
doing things, it's just that many of them won't take part in
all of the activities that a church has to undertake if it's going to do its job. They don't show up for meetings. We
have a great deal of committee work that has to be done,
but it's awfully hard to get anywhere when you have a no-
show attitude. People are very proud of their history here,
of Abe Lincoln, and we have a very good historical society,
but we don't always bring our history up-to-date by practicing the kind of things we did in the past. I don't think
there is the energy here that perhaps made this town a
little more progressive in the days when it was first founded.

"It's a great deal different here from the area in which
I had my church previously, in Wood River, Illinois, near
Alton, in the St. Louis area. We had a bigger population
and there was a much bigger influx of people. This is
where the big Shell and Standard Oil refineries are. So I
noticed a big difference in coming here."

Mr. Phillips says that his church tries to keep its members aware of things going on in the world. One program
was a six-week study of Latin American countries, part of
the church's missionary project. It was intended to attract
all ages. The participants would hold some meetings together and there would be missionaries to speak. There
were other activities directed to subjects outside the town.
"We've had a special Sunday on the United Nations. The
Social Relations Commission of the church has had programs on race relations problems. William Deems, the administrator of the new hospital, has spoken on the problems
of the aged. We've had a panel on political problems, con-
centrating especially on communism."

Had the church members spoken about the race relations problem insofar as the town was affected? "Well, we don't talk about Vandalia specifically. We talk about the need for understanding each other. We're trying to break down these prejudices in a general way, and engender an attitude of acceptance of the Negro, and we hope that by this sort of thing we can condition people to meet a situation with understanding when it finally develops." Mr. Phillips says also that they give money in their annual budget to the support of Methodist Negro colleges.

Mr. Phillips is a little frustrated at times: He is expected to be a chaplain, a marriage counselor, a public relations man, administrator, fund-raiser, educational director, visitor of the sick, etc. "There is enough work for an administrator to do eight hours a day. Then, of course, we have the hospital visits and counseling. There's very little time for studying and reading. We have our own district and conference meetings within the church organization. The minister has to be in back of practically everything in the town—attendance campaigns, canvasses for financial contributions. There's literature that has to be put out, special programs, special series of services that have to be done before Easter, and, of course, there's a man's wife and his children. [Mr. Phillips has three: seven, six, and four years old.] The church has 675 members, and when each one of them requires the sort of individual attention to all sorts of aspects of his life it's pretty hard to provide the kind of spiritual leadership a minister should give to his whole congregation. You almost have to administer to every person individually. I have a paid secretary, a custodian of the church, and a choir leader and an organist, but all the rest of the work falls on the minister. In the summer I have a youth director, but the youth director really is someone we ought to have all the year round. There just isn't anybody else to do all these things.

"Visiting the sick is a part of my work. The doctor helps physically, but people look to the minister for sympathy and understanding. The people are very insistent, we've found that out." Is this part of a minister's responsibility as a spiritual leader? "Yes. What is being a spiritual leader? It's to lead the people in our church to an experience with Christ. It's to teach them the Christian way of life. It's to bring them into the church and make them understand what is needed in order to live according to the Christian idea. That's what we were educated for in the seminary— to teach. That isn't really what seems to be mostly required of us now. The other things enter in."

Mr. Phillips admits that sometimes he strongly feels his inability to carry out his main function. He finds his reading interrupted with dozens of calls, and people dropping in just to pass the time of day. He sometimes wonders if his congregation wants the right things from him. "Sometimes a person's attitude will be that the only time I really need you is when I'm sick and if you don't come then you're not the kind of minister I want. The minister has very little defense against such demands. The problem isn't just in this church, it's one all the ministers have in town. Of course, if visiting a person when he is ill or providing other services helps to create a state of mind where he is willing to accept the church and learn a little bit more about the experience of Christianity, the minister is glad for the opportunity."

The young people are somewhat of a test for Mr. Phillips. There is the matter of the automobile and all the related things that go with it. "But we're not much different from other communities in that way. Our young people are pretty good in comparison with others. We don't have much juvenile delinquency, we don't have a lot of drinking. Maybe we don't know about it all, but we don't seem to have problems about sex with the younger people. The graduates from our high school who go to college are doing well in their education. They seem to be above the average in intelligence. But one of the things that disturbs me is the fact that the young people don't seem to take responsibility. I don't know if it's just this town, but my experience has been that you cannot depend on them as it seemed you could years ago. When you ask a youngster why he broke his promise to come to a meeting or to do something, and then didn't come, he shrugs, he gives some excuse such as his parents took him some place or he forgot, but he doesn't seem to be sorry or show any feeling of guilt. You'd think that he would be at least apologetic. I don't know what the reason for this attitude is, whether it's in our home or in our schools. You have to guide the high school children almost like grade school children. This is serious because this attitude has a great bearing on how these young people grow up and what they do with themselves later in life."

What do the young people want out of life? "Well, I think that the economic and security angle enters in much more than it should. Young people should try to develop a life for themselves, and making a life is not just getting a job that's important; it's developing a personality, becoming a person. Living depends on your whole being growing up, not just physically but spiritually. But the young people too often seem to think purely in terms of how do I get a job, what job brings the most money. We're just not made only to enjoy or feel comfortable."

Mr. Phillips and his wife recently took a church-sponsored trip to Washington, D.C., to learn about world affairs. They visited the State Department for briefings, the Pentagon, various embassies, the American University, and they heard some Congressmen and Senators. Last year they went to the UN in New York City. Mr. Phillip's congregation is always interested in hearing his reports on these trips, but he doesn't think people are very much alarmed about the condition the world is in.

When somebody had asked her about the world situation, Wanda McNary, the secretary of the Chamber of Commerce, had said that what the world needed was a real revival of religion. What did Mr. Phillips think religion could mean in terms of today's problems? Would it solve things? He answers that no religion has meaning unless you can get a commitment on the person's part. "If people were really committed to Christian behavior it would help keep families together, it would help us to live at peace with ourselves and our community, and if we're the kind of people that live at peace with ourselves, we'd be able much more to live at peace with the world. Religion isn't any magical dose. If you commit yourself to the Christian way it changes your life. It's a wrong notion to think that you can just pray and make things happen. Just being religious is not enough. Whatever you believe, or whatever you have of a religion, comes only through action and attitudes. There's no push-button solution to our problems, in religion or anything else." He quotes from Matthew, Chapter 7, Verse 21: "Not everyone that sayeth unto me, Lord, Lord, shall enter into the Kingdom of Heaven, but he that doeth the will of my Father, which is in Heaven."

THERE may be apathy and spiritual paralysis in other pews on Sunday, but Reverend Archie Brown's congregation, the largest in Vandalia, is a vigorous and dedicated army. The choir of the First Baptist Church is not the most sophisticated musical organization in town, but it sings with a happy heart. At the end of the sermon, Mr. Brown descends from his pulpit, stands amidst a congregation that packs the sanctuary, and calls for people to come down and show their willingness to join with God and church. On weekdays, Mr. Brown devotes his considerable energies to the proper functioning of that church. His office is in a new, three-story, brick Education Building adjoining the sanctuary. Mr. Brown is a man of medium height, with thick glasses and a calm, direct gaze. He talks in a distinctly unevangelistic tone of voice.

Mr. Brown is writing his eighth anniversary report. He previously had a church in Pinckneyville, nearby, and studied at the Southwestern Baptist Theological Seminary in Fort Worth, Texas. He is pleased with his present congregation.

"My church has given me fine support. I attended the Rural Baptist Alliance in London in 1955, and then went on a special trip to the Middle East and Rome. I went to the Baptist World Alliance in Rio de Janeiro, and took a tour of the mission field services we have in South America. The church also sent me to Alaska for three weeks, where I preached. One of the places was North Pole, Alaska. I have a family of two boys, who are grown, and one is trying the ministry. My congregation numbers 680 people, resident members, and 350 non-resident members who have moved away but who have not had their names taken off our rolls. We have an average of around 450 people— children and adults—who attend our Sunday school. Morning worship is usually attended by around 350 people, including some children.

"We are planning eventually to build a new sanctuary. Our Education Building was put up at a cost of $160,000. This was raised by the people of our congregation. Actually it is worth considerably more because much of the labor was donated. By 1960 we had reduced the debt to $19,000. On the other side of this building from the church we own the land to the corner, including the building on the corner. This set us back $90,000. The debt for this purchase of land is now down to $50,000. We are way ahead in the payments, and as soon as we can we will finance the sanctuary. We expect that a large chain store will lease the building on the other side of us, which is on our property.[3] We will remodel that building so that it will be suitable for a modern store. It will take four years to pay off what we will need to borrow in order to do the job. Then this will enable us to have the income to help pay the cost of our new sanctuary. We're paying $1,000 a month on our debt on the Education Building. Our budget is $61,900 a year, which is raised from the members of our congregation. The retirement of our debt on the Education Building is $12,375 a year.

"We have fine equipment here for our educational work. I use a tape recorder to record some of my broadcasts, which were heard for two years on the Effingham radio station. I think we have the best-equipped church of any around here for education. We have an electric typewriter, films, and an audio-visual system second to none, and a folding machine for our mailing. I know of no other church here that has a folding machine. We also have a modern filing system and a stenorette for secretarial work. Among our visual aids are a 16 mm. movie projector and a $500 screen and a slide projector.

"We have a large educational program. Sunday school is held in this building. We also have a training program for our teachers which meets at 6:30 every Sunday evening. It is graded according to age. We have the Women's Missionary Union, which has six circles. The young people's

---

[3] Since this interview the A&P agreed to lease the building.

mission work begins at the age of nine and goes right on up. We have a brotherhood program for men. The building is equipped to handle about 700 people. Of course, to get this many people in is like stacking hay in a barn, and we don't do it. We need more space in some parts of our program. For instance, we need three junior departments instead of two, we need four adult departments instead of three."

Hanging on the walls of the hallway outside Mr. Brown's office are four tiers of framed diplomas. These are Sunday school workers' diplomas, of four varieties, Mr. Brown explains. The first diploma, which is the ordinary one, is obtained when the teacher in training reads one book and spends ten hours of classwork on the book. On the diplomas are spaces for three colored seals, blue, red, and golden. A seal is obtained each time the diploma-holder reads another book and spends ten additional hours of work on that book in class. Then there is an "advanced" diploma, a "Master's" diploma, and, finally, a "Worker's Citation" diploma. To obtain all four diplomas with all twelve seals would require reading sixteen books and putting in ten hours on each book.

In another hallway is a visitational board, with a posted request to "Keep the Hangers Cleared." Mr. Brown says that when anyone misses two Sundays at Sunday school in a row, his name is put up on a card on the board. If he misses four successive Sundays, a red card is substituted, with the word "Danger" printed upon it. It is the responsibility of the teacher to take the card off the board and visit the truant at his home to find out the cause of the absence. The hangers are all "clear."

The second floor of the Education Building houses the nursery department. "We take people in here from birth to death," Mr. Brown explains. "Some people bring their babies to church two Sundays after the child is born." In the room called Nursery I, there are individual cribs and drawers under the cribs in which bottles and diapers can be placed. The beds are changed each time they are used and germicidal lamps kill any bacteria in the room. The various nursery rooms have had as many as seventy babies in them at a time. During church services they are attended by sitters. A public announcement system over the doorway of the nursery allows the sitters to hear Mr. Brown's sermon. All of the nursery rooms are air-conditioned. A closet in the hall contains a combination sink and stove, and an icebox with bottles of milk and graham crackers. After the nurseries come the classrooms for Beginners I and Beginners II, each holding around twenty-five to thirty children. Next to Beginners II is the classroom for Adults I, which adjoins the preacher's office and is also used for meetings of the church deacons. On the other floors are additional classrooms and assembly rooms, identified by such names as Junior I, Intermediate II, Primary I, Young People I, Adult III. Altogether the Education Building has sixty-five classrooms, large and small.

The church's educational program has been financed entirely by its congregation. "Our church as a whole stands very strongly on separation of church and state. We would not accept funds from the government," Mr. Brown says. "We feel the state's duty is to provide good public education. We'll take care of the religious education on Sunday and after school. We don't want government help, nor should any other denomination ask for tax money. If people want private schools and parochial schools, they should pay for it themselves." He adds that the Baptists have many hospitals, colleges, and seminaries, which have never accepted nor would accept federal money.

Mr. Brown sounds a bit nostalgic when discussing his mission as a spiritual leader. "There was a time when a pastor was called upon to preach Wednesdays and Sundays, conduct funerals, bring comfort to families of the deceased, visit the sick, and meet the spiritual needs of his community as best he could. Well, those days are gone forever. There's nothing more that a pastor would like than to be able to get back to that sort of thing. I like to preach the gospel and look after my church family. But today a pastor has to be an administrator. He has to take on a whole series of studies in church administration in the seminary. We've come to where we specialize. Every age group in our church has its educational program prepared by experts. We have to purchase literature, develop reading programs. We spend $400 a quarter just for literature. This is just a beginning. We have other books to buy too. Our training program is a big job. The pastor has much counseling to do. There are all kinds of problems brought up to us. There's the mixed-up child at school, there's the question of young people courting, what are the right things for them to do. Then there are couples ready to go on the rocks.

"My days begin at 6 o'clock in the morning. I come here at 7 and I don't get out of here until 10 or 11 o'clock at night most of the time. Then many times at night the phone will ring beside my bed and often I will go out and try to help somebody who is in difficulty.

"Then you have the problem of preparing yourself for the job as a spiritual leader. A pastor needs time to pray, much more time than he gets. Many pastors find trouble in having sufficient spiritual communion. Also, pastors are called upon to participate in community programs, community drives. I belong to the Rotary and Masons. I also help with the Red Cross drives, the bloodmobile, and so on. Of course, there are many things that the Chamber of Commerce wants to do to help the community, and I do what I can to cooperate. Then there is our responsibility to the school system. I want the faculty and the administration of our schools to know that I am interested, and that

I am trying to get my congregation to support the things they are trying to do. You are expected to attend sporting and entertainment events, which quicken the child's interest in his school. There's no end to these things.

"Then of course I have responsibilities to the church outside my community. I am chairman of the Board of Directors of the Illinois Baptist State Association. I'm also on the Board of Directors of the Southwest Baptist Theological Seminary in Fort Worth. I write a Sunday lesson that appears weekly in the local paper, and I have written a book and hope to write another. The book I have written is called *A Million Men for Christ,* and it describes the work and purpose of the Baptist Church. Of course, I am helped a great deal by committees. I couldn't do all of these things by myself.

"Sometimes people ask me, how do you Baptists do all you do? We do not have lots of wealth, but we have people who believe in Christianity and are willing to make sacrifices. We encourage them to give a tithe or more. Of course, many people give nothing, but others are extremely conscientious about their contributions. We keep as good a set of books as any business you find. We give our members a monthly record of their contributions to the church which they can use for income-tax purposes. We have a secretary here on part-time to handle just financial affairs. Twenty per cent of our budget goes to support foreign missions. We hope to increase this support. Then we have home missions. In Illinois we estimate that there is one new Southern Baptist church every ten days. I look forward to the time when we could have nearly 1,000 Southern Baptist churches in Chicago alone, where there is a great increase in population."

Since a good percentage of Chicago's population increase is Negro, what is the situation with regard to Negro memberships in the Baptist churches? Mr. Brown says one

Baptist pastor cannot speak for others. "You must think of the Baptist Church as a local church. We have an association of churches, or a convention, but we run in a very democratic way. There are no decrees by one group of Baptists that bind any other Baptist churches. The individual church decides its own positions. Nobody can interfere with our property or the way we conduct ourselves. The congregation elects its own ministers. Everybody in the congregation votes. The majority rules."

Mr. Brown says his own feelings about the Negro must go back to his own boyhood. He was born and raised in Harrisburg, Illinois, where there were many Negroes. "They attended school with us. When I graduated I sat by a Negro. I played football on the same team with Negroes. They have every right I have. They ought to be given every privilege of education and employment and citizenship that any citizen has a right to expect. What would I do if a Negro presented himself for church membership? I would do what the congregation says it wants to do. Many people in this congregation might resign if a Negro were admitted, but I hope that a majority would support a membership application. In other cities Negroes have been refused membership, generally not on the grounds of their race, but because their applications for membership were artificial and attempts to test a congregation's attitude.

"When I was pastor in Pinckneyville, they had an unwritten rule that no Negroes should be in town after sundown. No Negroes could live in the community. I don't agree with this attitude. I think with the younger generation the picture is changing. If a Negro family came to our church to attend services it would be seated in this church. I cannot say what would happen if they came to join and asked for membership. It would be a problem, which would eventually be decided by the congregation.

"The procedure for a Negro would be the same as for

any other person. He would present himself for church membership. Then he would meet with the deacons, of which we have twenty-three, and there would be a discussion. The deacons would ask him about his motives in joining. Then the deacons would make a recommendation to the congregation. These recommendations are ordinarily followed. However, there would be an open discussion at the monthly business meeting of the congregation, when the recommendation was brought up. I would make my views clear."

ANOTHER minister who has the habit of making his views clear, and who, like Mr. Brown, keeps in close touch with everything going on in town, is Ralph Smith, the Presbyterian minister. He is a handsome, young, dark-haired man who has a number of ideas that some old-time Vandalians feel must have been imported from Ohio. His political instincts are lively enough to have already qualified him for a three-hour visit from Illinois's most earnest and patriotic mind-inspector, State Senator Paul Broyles, who wanted to know why Mr. Smith has taken it upon himself to raise questions about the value of such established institutions as the House Un-American Activities Committee.

It has already been mentioned that Mr. Smith has caused the community air to vibrate by bringing up the matter of discrimination against Negroes. His Race Relations Sunday sermon last winter began in the following manner: "Sit-ins and freedom riders remind us that somewhere in the land there is hatred and violence erupting. Our first reaction may be that of condemnation toward those who stir up all this trouble. Why can't they be happy with what they've got? Our next reaction may be that of relief, as we thank God that we don't have any problems like that in peaceful Vandalia. We're thankful that we're an integrated

community here. After all, we do have a Negro family in
the county. There is at least one Negro child in our school
system. We're proud that there's never been any violence
or commotion over our integration.

"Well, now, you know as well as I do that if we take this
attitude seriously we're not kidding anybody but ourselves.
In the United States there are approximately 16,000,000
Negroes. That's about 10 per cent of the population. In
Fayette County there are less than ten Negro residents.
That figures out not to 1 per cent, not to 1/100 of 1 per
cent, but to 5/10,000 of 1 per cent. If you can imagine a
scale 20 inches high representing the national percentage
of Negro Americans, then the percentage of Negroes in
Fayette County would have to be represented by a height
the thickness of one piece of cigarette paper.

"Now why are these scales so disproportionate? Why is
there such a small number of Negroes in our community?
You know the answer. We don't want them. We have an
unwritten law that says that when sundown comes they had
best be on their way. They can't stay in the hotels, there
are only two motels where they are welcome, and if a Negro
would insist on buying a house in town here, heaven only
knows what would happen to him.

"The only way this unwritten law and these attitudes
can remain is when they have the sanction and backing of
the citizens."

Complacency and downright "laziness in the pews," as
one of Mr. Smith's visiting pastors, the Reverend Christos
Vais puts it, are two other subjects that crop up frequently
in Mr. Smith's conversation.

"Yes, Vandalia is a pretty good town. Of course, some of
us live with women not our wives, we cheat on our taxes,
but we don't knife each other, we don't have dope. People
don't go hungry here.

"We have our share of viciousness, but when you're down most people are willing to come and give you a hand up. Maybe this is because they get a certain enjoyment from grouping about you and being protective. People here don't see the world outside Vandalia as having anything to do with them. They are concerned with their work and their income and their children. We seek security and we find it here. Perhaps if John Birchers did make an approach they'd get a few local helpers. This is a very quiet, stable community. The drugstores sell a lot of tranquilizers.

"We ought to do more to help ourselves. We could make a junior college out of the State House instead of keeping it there as an empty museum. In some ways, in the past there's been too much leadership. It tends to make us flaccid. The citizens didn't build their library, it was given to them. The parks and recreational areas were given.

"There are two power groups here. One is the city officials, they're elected. If you want something done in terms of a drive, then, of course, you have to get their clearance and support. Then there's the other power group which is in the background. These are some of the very old and established citizens, some of them millionaires. It is very important that they not be opposed to what you want to do.[4]

---

[4] *Cf.* Father Francis Gribbin: "There is a quantity of the more wealthy people who dominate the town. The ordinary people don't get far with them. These wealthy people control. They are filled up with the idea that people should play to them. They expect to be looked up to. But they are not looked up to. The common people here would like to move forward. There's nothing to move forward with. The old gang still runs the Chamber of Commerce. The Junior Chamber is in a struggling state. The only hope they have is that the domineering class will be defeated. The domineering comes from a long time back. They are continually in concert with each other. The harmony is all a set-up. Most of these fellows acquired money when things were at a low ebb, and now they are in a position of control. Most of them are in businesses. They look out for each other. You boost me and I'll boost you. It'll take a long time to break this."

"Culturally we can be doing much better. The high school has a tremendous gym, but it doesn't even have an auditorium where there could be theatre performances, either by high school groups or by outside groups, or concerts. Of course, we have the Navy Band, and we also have Anna Ruth Kains with her Messiah Choir at Christmas, which is the great event, and the high school band gives concerts in the summer. But if you ask anybody about Beethoven or something about philosophy, you get a blank look.

"The church has ceased to be the center of social activity in this community. I guess this is true in a lot of other places too. It's competing with school activities. Then there is the automobile, of course. You've heard about this from the school people. A car is an escape. The young people want to get away from home. This is true of America in general, it's not just the families around here.

"However, we are having good success with our young people in our church school. We have a program called 'Christian Faith and Life.' It's the standard Presbyterian curriculum. Books are provided for the juniors on up in the school. They are hard-cover books which the children are allowed to keep. Attendance is up. There is some opposition to this program in the congregation. It costs more money, but not a great deal more money. The budget for Christian education in 1960 was $500, last year $700."

Mr. Smith has 226 in his congregation, with an average attendance of 100 people on a Sunday. "The Lutherans cut off the dead wood. Church membership is a sacred thing to them. They don't tolerate inactive members. This seems right. When you go to church, you promise to follow God and attend church. The church has the responsibility to bring you back if you don't attend, of course. I know one person who hasn't been in our Presbyterian church for two years. By not coming back he's broken his promise, and he should be suspended. But most churches don't do this."

Mr. Smith has definite ideas about where his responsibility to the congregation begins and ends. He feels that too many pastors take on jobs that ought to be performed by the congregation committees. Shortly after Mr. Smith's installation the lights burned for three days in his church. A parishioner finally called the matter to his attention, saying that the previous pastor had always taken care of such things. Mr. Smith replied that from now on his congregation committees would see to it that the windows were closed, the coal ordered, and the lights turned off, and he would preach the sermons and perform the weddings.

What should a minister do if his congregation refused to admit a Negro family? His first feeling is that the minister should shake the dust of the town from his feet. On second thought he thinks that a pastor who resigns on such an issue might be taking the easy way out. "Shouldn't the pastor try to work with the congregation and bring it around to his way of thinking? Shouldn't he say, 'This is where I am needed because there are un-Christian attitudes?' Should a pastor work only with congregations that agree with him? Where is the point at which a pastor resigns? How long, oh Lord, how long?"

Ralph Smith and Archie Brown share the dilemma.

VII

: At some point, obviously, talks end. They leave an outsider with the feeling that, with all the glimpses he has had of the town, of people, of ideas, he has spent most of his time traveling across intersections and looking down roadways he will never have the chance to follow. At the beginning of the exploration the pictures emerge fresh and uncomplicated, but as the talk accumulates, lines blur and some of the freshness dies out of the colors. There is no sense in trying to pile collections of impressions or ideas on top of each other to get some generalization that applies especially to Vandalia. Then whatever substance individual conversations may have had is completely lost. Vandalians are not to be melted down into some average piece of something any more readily than anybody else, nor is the town they live in explained as the sum of everything they say about it or want it to be.

The corporation of Vandalia is an aggregate of people and properties, but as a community it is nothing more or less than a single idea, very personal and private, in the mind of each of its citizens. Perhaps someone could draw a composite face of all of them if he were to tailor his questions carefully, but there would be no features in the face. Vandalia is not a place to find a "community attitude," which is probably what Judge Burnside means when he makes the remark, "We're not any special sort of a town. People come here from all over," silently adding that this is where their ideas come from, too.

If the people of Vandalia are not entirely unlike other Americans, there may be some importance in the conclusion that they do not have established sets of ideas, even though they may observe fairly rigid rules of social conduct and share a common vocabulary of stock phrases. It can be argued that this is not a discovery, that it is obvious, and that the people of no community—not even in Puritan New England—ever really had a set of standard thoughts, no matter how total the conformity was on the surface. Even if this argument is granted, the people of Vandalia hardly fit into the Main Street folklore which has been built up around the rural Midwestern town. At least when they are pressed they express self-criticism and lively dissent, and anyone who expects to hear them talk like the people of Sinclair Lewis's Sauk Center will either have to ignore half of what he hears or take charge of the conversations and drive them in the direction he believes they ought to take.

The talks in Vandalia do not support the American myth that a rural town today is a land-locked island inhabited by people who share an abiding complacency with each other. There are the surface appearances of unity and its concomitant sterility in Vandalia, and the appearances are sometimes overwhelming. But they do not persist in the face of its own citizens' conflicting testimony. Vandalians today are in some ways in a better position to observe and to feel, sometimes most painfully, the consequences of a changing society than the suburbanite who lives in a bedroom town or the city dweller who hears about the world mainly from his newspaper and who enjoys the protective layers afforded him by his corporation, his union, and his various other institutional affiliations. There is also a special urgency in the air of Vandalia. A town on the edge of Chicago, Los Angeles, or New York City is forced to deal with the problems of sudden and uncontrolled growth, but Vandalia is beset by the much more desperate problem of how to hold on to what it has in order to survive.

Security is not one of the values the townspeople attach to living in their community. Vandalia families cannot be certain about the future of their community or even of their ability to remain in it. The favorable employment statistics in the Chamber of Commerce's brochure do not veil the fact that jobs now held are in constant danger of disappearing, whether they are in the factory, farm, or local store, and that a great percentage of them cannot support a family or offer any hope for advancement. The family that wants to remain in Vandalia, far from being insulated from the tensions and threats of the outer world, is resisting economic, social, and technological forces that could break the community apart and send the pieces flying in all directions.

Whereas many Americans live in or around the great cities unwillingly because that is where the jobs are, Vandalians live in their town because they want to. Their reasons are not new, but they have an added poignance because the things these people value are becoming harder to hold on to. They like the freedom of association and personal trust they do not believe can be found in a large city. They hope to maintain a school system in which their children receive a common educational experience in small classes with good teachers. Perhaps, as William Deems says, there is something unhealthy about the way Vandalians meet each local problem with a fund drive; nevertheless, they esteem the relationships with each other that make such solutions practicable.

There are many reasons why a man stays in Vandalia when, as Joe Dees puts it, "he could get the paid vacations and fringe benefits in the city," and most of them recur over and over in the talks. Underlying them all seems to be a desire to be able to know the whole of one's town, to be "some kind of a somebody" in it, to be able to circulate in it freely, and to be part of a social arrangement where there are certain justified assumptions about how people will deal with each other. On a freezing day, Mrs. Mark Miller is operating under one of these assumptions when she asks the postmaster who has just sold her some stamps to call a taxi for her. There is nothing trivial about the transaction.

Vandalia's lawyers and doctors and farmers and teachers and businessmen have their difficulties in talking about what they believe themselves and their community to be. Some of their trouble comes from an unconscious absorption of many of the standard myths about small-town complacency, neighborliness, Godliness, stupidity, provincialism, loyalties, unity, freshness. A tale heard often enough sometimes becomes part of the conversation, and a Vandalian does not usually speak of his community without himself introducing some of the stereotyped criticisms. The view that talks with people in their own environment will dispel the myth of their environment can be misleading.

Despite all their advertised contact with their fellow human beings, many Vandalians seem to do much of their thinking in isolation. Perhaps it is because their problems are so closely bound up with personal relationships that many of them are less inclined to speak openly about them. In a community where almost everyone knows everyone else by name and face, and converses with ease and frequency, the citizens for the most part exchange commonplaces. Dan Hockman, a high school history teacher, describes the situation when he says, "People here are interested in what other people are up to, not in what they

think." With all their togetherness—the word is not used
with disdain—there are many, many isolated people in the
community. Sometimes the isolation is by choice. Alenia
McCord says apologetically, "We have our standards and
we tend to be a little intolerant of other people if they
don't agree with us, but we don't try to railroad our standards on others. If somebody doesn't come up to our standards that's all right just as long as they keep a long distance
away from us." More often, however, the isolation is
neither sought nor enjoyed. Conversations on the most
affecting personal and intellectual matters are given freely
—to the outsider who asks for them—but when the conversations end, sometimes after many hours of intense exchange, the conclusion is very often a wish that it might
happen again and a remark that it almost never happened
before.

Perhaps the absence of serious talk with others in their
community explains why so many of the townspeople combine their own inner guesses with mixtures of the prevalent
myths, and thereby supplement the myths. There are many
remarks about the curse of complacency in the town and,
taken together, the people who are disturbed about it make
up a sizable portion of the population. But, like the Reverend Ralph Smith, they are really annoyed at the nature
of the peace, not the peace itself, at the inertia that seems to
be responsible for the lack of conflict and motion in the
community. If the inertia proceeds from smugness and total
satisfaction with the past, anything Mr. Smith has to say
in criticism of "Peaceful Valley" seems relatively mild. But
if the inertia grows out of confusion and bewilderment,
and the clinging to tradition is done in desperation, then
Mr. Smith is being harsh, because the peace in the valley
is a troubled one.

It is strange to discover that an assembly of people who

live together with a decency unheard of in a large city, and whose community efforts have been astonishingly successful, should at the same time lack the sort of serious communication with each other that would seem to be the basis of democratic life. The potential exists. Vandalia has an unusual assortment of sensitive and informed people. They have opinions, ideas, tempers. The would like to make their town better. But, given this, there is a reticence on important matters that is forbidding, and a lack of a forum— a New England-style town meeting, for instance—in which regular discussions could proceed.

In some ways, Vandalians leave the impression that they are members of a family in which the main strength of the past has become a problem for the future. They have had the advantage of similar origins and close kinship, but perhaps so close that, as the family grows and disperses, too much of the dependency remains. And, like a family, they have lived and talked with each other steadily over the years but have kept their real thoughts and worries about each other inside. The old bonds that held Vandalia in a sort of perpetual stability are breaking. There are many departures from the family and few arrivals.

If there is to be a new way for the town, it has many assets which do not appear in Robert Hasler's typewritten town biography. Vandalia is not condemned to become a suburb of anything just yet, and it still has transportation facilities that can serve whatever new industrial establishments it may attract. One advantage of its unhurried history is that no huge defense plants have dropped down on the town to crush its character forever and then move on in a few years. Vandalia has natural beauties that make it a place apart. Few towns to the north have spreading elms and maples of such beauty, and in May there is the wild spring blaze of lilac and dogwood. The Kaskaskia is a navigator's nightmare now, but in a few years flood-control dams below and above Vandalia will reclaim much valuable farm land, and, not incidentally, provide fishing and boating for local boys and girls and out-of-state tourists.

Obviously, what happens in Vandalia depends on the people who will have to manage these assets, and what improvements they make in their present arrangements of organizing themselves and communicating with each other. One cannot really tell how they will do, even after talking to them for a long, long time. Affairs move slowly. But there are stirrings and there are contradictions. Judge Burnside says nobody pays any attention to the railroads. On the other hand, in his church by the railroad, Mr. Smith has to stop in the middle of his Sunday sermon when he hears the "Spirit of St. Louis" coming down the tracks.

About the Author

Joseph Lyford, 45, spent his boyhood in a small Illinois town. He has been a professional journalist for nearly twenty-five years. At Harvard he was an editor of the *Crimson,* and a regular reporter on the Boston *Post.* At one point in his Navy service in World War II, he wrote and broadcast a radio-newspaper, the New Georgia *Daily Tribune* in the Solomon Islands. Later he was public information officer for the U.S. Seventh Fleet and wrote extensively for the English language press in Shanghai, and the Shanghai and Tokyo editions of *The Stars and Stripes.*

After the war Mr. Lyford worked on the foreign desk of International News Service, then as an assistant editor on the *New Republic.* In 1948 he was appointed press secretary to Governor Chester Bowles of Connecticut. Two years later he directed the successful election campaign of U.S. Senator William Benton. After a year as European correspondent for the Hartford *Times,* he ran unsuccessfully for the U.S. House of Representatives from Connecticut's Fourth District. In 1954 he ran for Congressman-at-large, and was narrowly defeated. During this period, Lyford was staff director for the Public Education Association of New York City. Since 1955 he has been a staff member of the Fund for the Republic.

The author lives on the West Side of Manhattan in New York City with his wife, Jean, a school teacher, and infant daughter, Amy. He is preparing a book on the life of Puerto Ricans, Negroes, and whites in his community. Mr. Lyford is a member of his local school board.

Previous books by Mr. Lyford include *Candidate* and *The Agreeable Autocracies.* He has contributed to *Saturday Review, The New Republic, America,* and the *Bulletin* of the American Association of University Professors. The Fund for the Republic has published one of his essays in its pamphlet *The Negro as an American.* Mr. Lyford has produced several studies of the press, including a report on foreign news coverage published by the International Press Institute; *The New York Times and Latin America* (a Fund study); and, with Louis J. Lyons, a curator of Harvard's Nieman Foundation for Journalism, *The Press and the People,* a national television series which won a citation from the Overseas Press Club.

HARPER COLOPHON BOOKS